Carry on Castle

A memoir about fairytale love,
sudden, unexpected death,
and the penetrating grief.

By
Jennifer Stults

*This book is
dedicated to:*

Dan Stults

*All my love,
all my life*

Thank you to my editors:

Stacie Gordon
and
Kurt Schumacher

For making it a readable book

Contents

FOREWARD:

How do I heal my heart? Tell your story

∞ ∞ ∞

Every story is connected
Each one to another
Part of your story is some of my story
And a little bit of every other

One day my story I'll tell to you
Just as the author intended
Without abridgement or addition
Completely unimpeded

Dan Stults

This starts as a love story. True love. Fairy tale love. A love most people only dream of. I had it. I was living my happily ever after with my prince. I think that story, in itself, would make a great Nicholas Sparks movie.

Then the story changed, it had the most unexpected twist that blew the entire audience away. Out of nowhere, the beautiful love story turned into a nightmare.

I was 34 when my husband, Dan, had a seizure and was pronounced dead on our living room floor at 12:01 AM on January 12, 2015. Just six weeks earlier, he had turned 36. Our daughter was 7 ½ years old, and we were in the process of adopting a baby. We had been married for 15 years. We were high school sweethearts who met at church camp. I was 16 when Dan declared that, "Sometime between the first time I saw her and the very next breath I took, I fell in love." We had our whole lives ahead of us, but in an instant, it was all over. My husband stopped breathing. I, however, continue to breathe. Our daughter continues to breathe. As excruciating as it is, we still breathe.

Is this a story about my grief experience or my true love? I wouldn't have this grief if not for the fairytale love I had. "This isn't my life. This isn't what happens to me," I said out loud for weeks after he died. I mumbled it under my breath for months. I screamed it to my dad the night my husband died, and I told it to over 400 people at his funeral. I've been living in a life that isn't mine for three years now and I still think this every day.

I first started writing about my grief for one simple reason: I wanted to SLEEP. After my husband died in the middle of the night, it seemed impossible for me to fall asleep. I would just lie in bed and think about him. I would think about him dying, think about him smiling, think about all the things we had done and all the things we would never do. Sleep seemed impossible. My therapist suggested that I start a blog. Maybe I could fall asleep if I could get all those thoughts out of my head. So, I did. It definitely helped with the sleeping, although it wasn't perfect. As a side effect, it turned out that people could relate to my writing and, to my amazement, seemed to like it. My family and friends seem to love it, but they have been so supportive of me in this whole thing, that I'm pretty sure at this point I could pick my nose and they would say, "Good job Jenny, that was great nose picking." Not that that is a bad thing; their support has been astronomical and so needed. I'm just saying I think their opinions are a little biased.

I believe what people like about it is I tell the truth. I tell the truth about grief as I know it, and people have responded to it. I never imagined I would write a book. I never imagined I would be a 34-year-old widow either, but here I am.

I have discovered that I have a story to tell: about Dan, about our love, about his sudden and unexpected death, about our daughter's grief and my own. I am 38 and the solo parent of an eleven-year-old girl named India. As much as I don't want to be here, I AM here: in a life that never was supposed to happen, and that I don't want. However, one of the things I tell people is that I wasn't given a choice. None of us were given a choice. We are still alive, and we have no choice but to carry on.

I never in my life considered writing a book. Writing wasn't my thing; it was Dan's thing. However, I can't get this story out of my head so I'm writing it down. Maybe it will help other people sleep, maybe it will help them see they are not going crazy, they are just grieving, and maybe it will give non-grievers some perspective.

Also I named all my chapters after lines from the musical Hamilton, because I love it.

> *If you have ever lost a loved one, then you know exactly how it feels. And if you have not, then you cannot possibly imagine it.*
> — Lemony Snicket, *The Bad Beginning*

CHAPTER 1:

Who lives, who dies, who tells your story

∞ ∞ ∞

I will never love anything more in this world than I loved him.

— *Buffy the Vampire Slayer*

Dan was a writer. He wanted to write counseling books, theology books, parenting books, children's books, and young adult novels. It reminds me of that Hamilton line: "Why do you write like you're running out of time? Write day and night like your writing out of time?" Dan was always writing. He always had something to write about and at least 100 more ideas in his head of things to write about when he could find the time.

Dan wrote out his three main goals in life:

My first goal is to love. I want to love God with all my heart, mind, and soul. I find this daunting, and I challenge anyone who doesn't. "Heart, mind, and soul" is basically symbolic, representing the whole of one's being. No compartmentalizing, only holistic, unhindered love. I don't do it, but this is my goal. I want to love my family. Despite my many foibles and failings, I really, truly, really want to be a better father and a better husband every day. I want to love them more deeply every day. I want to submit and support, lead and guide, follow and encourage. I want to love my friends. I want to be a support, I want to build up, I want to cheer on. I want to know and be known in a personal, transparent way that opens me up and opens them up to compliments and critique, accolades and accountability. I want to love others. I want to show compassion, empathy, and aid to those who need it. I want to be a safe place for people in a dangerous world. I want to figure out what it means to be incarnational. I want to love my enemies. I want to not be overcome by evil, but overcome evil with good (this is a hard one for me, I'm pretty vengeful). I want them to be so surprised, so taken aback, so shocked by my love in the face of their, well, enemyness, that the seeds of revolution will be planted in their heart.

My second goal is life. There is so much to see, so much to do, so much to experience. There are so many blessings to give and receive and I don't want to miss it. I don't want to look back on anything with regret, I don't want to wish I had been brave or bold. This is difficult for me as I am pretty much always shy and sometimes cowardly. I am frustrated by the human tendency to get stuck doing things a certain way because they have always been done that way or to think that something can't be done simply because it has never been done before. When St. Peter meets me at the pearly gates and introduces me to my first angel, and that angel asks me, "So, what is life like?" I want to have a good answer.

My third goal is to leave a legacy. Our lives are but mist, or the equivalent of the blink of an eye in all of time. We will not be around very long and we will not be remembered. Almost everything we do, even the most powerful and influential of us, fades away into meaninglessness and is without consequence. Almost. Some people live their whole lives like this and simply don't care and it drives me insane. I want to leave a legacy; I want the time allotted to me to result in more than consumed resources and over-populating offspring. I want said offspring to know me, to know their history through me. I want lives and subsequent generations to be different because I was involved. I want to help people heal and be transformed now and after I meet that angel. Lofty and perhaps a little arrogant? Yeah, probably, but also doable.

Dan was the Lorax. He spoke for the trees. His favorite phrase comes from *The Lorax*: "Unless someone like you cares a whole awful lot, nothing is going to get better. It's not." Dan was that someone that cared a whole awful lot, someone that cared enough to make it better. An avid environmentalist, he was always trying to save the planet. When he was a kid, he built a wildlife habitat in his back yard. He would get mad at his dad for trimming trees. "You cut too much down. The earth needs trees." He wanted to be part of the ASPCA saving animals wherever he could. He was big on animal rights, and rescuing animals that needed a home. We ended up with three cats, two bunnies, a rat, and a tarantula that way. I drew the line at a pig, but he tried.

Dan was a counselor. it wasn't just his job, it was who he was. It was just part of his being. Even in high school friends would come to him for a listening ear and some advice. Everyone knew if you had a problem to go talk to Dan about it. I wonder what percentage of his job was counseling actual clients verses other staff members.

I bet it's pretty close to 50/50. Even my sisters and his mom would get advice about life from him. That is who Dan was.

Our daughter India had him wrapped around her little finger from the moment she was conceived. He treated India like she was the most precious thing in the world, because to us she was. He would dance and sing with her. He would make up songs on the spot. Once they made up an opera together, and I was lucky enough to catch it on video.

I couldn't wait for him to get home from work every day. To give him an "I'm glad you're home" kiss. I felt completely safe and secure when he was around. I didn't realize how much until he was gone and I didn't have that feeling of safety anymore.

Dan's friend Esther told me once, "You know, Dan would light up when he talked about you. He thought you were amazing. You could tell by his body language how wonderful he thought you were."

Dan did think I was amazing. I could never figure out why, but I knew he thought it. He told me every day how wonderful I was. I would make some crafty little project and he would be blown away. He was in awe of our family scrapbooks, assuring me he could never make anything like that. He was continually amazed at how I did things right under his nose.

When people asked me about getting things fixed around my house I always said "Well, Dan is what one would call an intellectual. Dan is not a handyman." I was more of a handyman than Dan was. Dan couldn't fix anything. In fact, Dan sucked at fixing stuff. I fixed all our stuff. Not that I did a fabulous job at it or anything, but it was better than what Dan could have done. Dan could change a tire if he had to, but frankly, he would rather call AAA. Dan was very, very, very smart. Dan could not fix anything.

Yet still, we shared responsibilities equally. We never fought, we never yelled at each other. That just wasn't our way. When we would disagree, it would end in laughter.

It was always the two of us against whatever may come. My friend Jill wrote to me once about what she thought of our relationship:

> He was a full partner. I mean every relationship has its dynamics, even family ones. But you were partners. I always wanted that kind of relationship and watching you two as a single person gave me some hope. The only words I have for it are "partner' and "team". But that is so weak; it just hits the surface. He wasn't a sit back and do his own thing guy. Neither were you.

Yes, that was us. We were 100% in this together.

One time, I was asked in an interview what would I say my husband's biggest flaw was. I looked her straight in the eye and very seriously I said, "He procrastinates like there's no tomorrow." To me, that was my husband's greatest flaw. It really was the very worst thing about him. He would pack his bag ten minutes before leaving for the airport. Mine would be done the day before. He was the guy that wrote sermons on a napkin in the car on the way to church. At least I was driving! Those were some of his best sermons too. Dan was not lazy, but he did procrastinate so much he could be perceived as lazy. He liked to tell me that, when I would ask him if he had finished some project. "Well right now, Jennifer, I'm being perceived as lazy." All I could do was shake my head at him. I would give anything to have him here doing any one of those things again. Even annoyances are missed when they are gone forever.

Dan hated mint. I love mint. He hated it so much that he wouldn't kiss me if I had eaten anything with mint. He hated mint so much that he would use children's fruity toothpaste. Mint mochas are one of my favorites, and he hated them. But it wouldn't stop him from bringing me one home from Starbucks when I was having a hard day. It didn't stop him from making me a homemade one and bringing it to me as I cuddled our daughter on the couch.

He was incredibly disorganized. He liked to call me his personal secretary because I was always finding his stuff for him: socks, keys, milk. He used to open the fridge door and say, "Jennifer, I can't find the milk!" I would go into the kitchen to look and there was the milk in the fridge, right in front of his eyes, but he didn't see it.

Along with his disorganization came his complete lack of direction. Dan was always getting lost. So much so that when he would come home late from work, I would tease, "What happened did you get lost?" He once got lost going to the city library. He once got lost going to my parents' house from his parents' house. Dan was so excited when they invented GPS. It was one of the best things that ever happened to him. Sometimes, though, he would still get lost anyway.

Dan hoarded papers. Every article he found, every workshop he went to, every paper he received in class, every paper he wrote, stories, poems. He kept it all. We had stacks and stacks of papers all over our house. I would try to organize them for him, but it was a pointless endeavor. Every time I turned around, there were more papers. Yet every time he needed a specific one, I was able to find it for him.

I think Dan loved me more than anyone has ever loved someone before. You could say he spoiled me, but that was just his love spilling over in physical ways. He always woke up earlier then me and would turn on the heat, so the house would be warm when I got out of bed. He would bring the groceries in from the car for me. He would set the alarm every night; I never had to worry about doing it. He would walk through the house every night and make sure everything was locked and turned off. He would haul all our holiday decorations to and from the shed. He would make me baths; with bubbles and salts and candles; without me ever asking; he could just tell that I needed one. He would wash my hair for me when I was having a bad day. He would sleep with his hand on my hip. "God made us so my hand fits perfectly on your hip," he would say. He would hold my hand all the time, even after 15 years of marriage. He would bring me Tylenol and Sudafed when I was sick; he just knew I needed it and I hadn't taken it on my own. He would bring me warm socks; he could just tell my feet were cold. At restaurants, he always ordered something he knew I would like so he could trade with me if I didn't like what I ordered. This turned out to be the case frequently. Dan was the only one who always called me Jennifer. He thought it was beautiful and elegant. Everyone else calls me Jenny.

Until the day he died, Dan put other people before himself: all other people. It didn't matter if you were his brother, his mother, a random kid at church, a homeless person on the street, someone who was mentally ill, or his wife and daughter. Dan was always more concerned about others' wellbeing than his own. A friend of ours wrote about Dan:

> Dan was always ready to defend the weak and offer love in the face of dogmatism, fear, and bigotry. In the evangelical Christian world I grew up in, where "love" is usually prefaced by "tough" and hating the sin is more important than loving the sinner, Dan stood out in stark contrast.
>
> One night after youth group, Dan and another youth pastor took a small group of kids, myself included, into downtown Boise to meet the homeless teens he was helping. That night, Dan did something very small, very insignificant that changed my worldview and influenced

*how I have interacted with homeless and downtrodden
people ever since.*

*What did he do, you may ask? Only this: He took out a
cigarette lighter and lit the cigarette of a person who
wanted to smoke. He didn't make a fuss about it, many
people probably would not have noticed it, but I did. Dan
was not a smoker. He carried the lighter because he
wanted to be the friend who offered a light in the
darkness.*

*To be clear, Dan was not advocating smoking; if any of
these kids had wanted to quit smoking he would have been
the first to offer help. He did this in order to meet people
where they were at, not where he thought they ought to
be.*

Dan did not "love the sinner, hate the sin". He did not even
"love the sinner". He just loved. Full stop. Without exception and
without caveat.

Dan wrote once:

*I believe in compassion as one of the highest virtues one
can strive for... I have subsequently learned that the wise
thing to do is look for God in every person I interact with
and every occasion I find myself in. Time and again God
humbles me by allowing me a glimpse of himself where I
least expect it-in the tears of an oppositional defiant child,
in the clingy behavior of his dependent mother, even in the
delusions of a profoundly mentally ill man who just talked
to Jesus the night before.*

That's just how he viewed the world. I don't know if I know of
anyone more self-sacrificing then Dan. Perhaps in movies or
famous people like Mother Theresa, but in my own little circle of
the world it was Dan. He was the guy that would give you the shirt

off his back; I have literally seen him do just that several times. He was the guy that, when I was worried about how broke we were, was donating money to causes because he felt they needed it more than we did. He came home once with no shoes because he met someone that didn't have any and he had more in his closet. He never worried about himself or what he needed or even wanted, except for the occasional tattoo. He was way more concerned about helping others or spoiling India and me.

Dan was doing so much good in the world, and he could have done so much more. At his funeral I ended my eulogy by saying,

> *Every day that you saw Dan you witnessed love, and*
> *your lives were better for it.*

In The Princess Bride, Wesley declares, "Death cannot stop true love." I used to wholeheartedly agree with. Yes! Death cannot stop true love. If you truly love someone, death will not and cannot stop you from being together. Just look at Wesley and Buttercup! Death didn't stop them. That was Dan and me. We had true love forever. Death would not stop us from our love; we would find a way around it. Then Dan had a seizure one night and died. Just died, out of nowhere. His boat wasn't captured by pirates, although I'm sure he would have preferred to go out that way. Even now, I am hoping he can come back, that it was all some huge mistake, that the evil villain told me he was dead, but really he was taking over the ship, building immunity to iocane powder, and on his way back to me. Death cannot stop our love.

Yes, I hate that line. Dan's dead for real, not like in a fairy tale where there is some loophole, this is real life. As much as we loved each other, he died anyway.

CHAPTER 2:

Look Around at How Lucky We Are to be Alive Right Now

∞ ∞ ∞

Dan always said, "It wasn't love at first sight, but sometime between the first time I saw her and the very next breath I took that I fell in love." Many years later he said in describing himself "I am a husband; one of the greatest joys in my life is simply making my wife smile."

Dan and I met at one of the most beautiful places in Oregon; it's right on a lake covered in evergreen trees, but a short hike over the dunes puts you on the beach. It just so happened that it was a church camp. We had worship with cool nineties songs by Newsboys, D.C. Talk, and (Dan's all-time favorite band) Third Day. We hung out and played games, talked a lot about this Jesus guy, and walked on the beach. They wouldn't let us swim in the ocean, something about safety, but there were camp fires every night. Oh yeah, and I met my soulmate. It was a pretty good camp.

I can remember the first time I ever saw him. I was 16 years old. I was sitting on top of a picnic table (I was a rebel like that) near the lake. A bunch of friends were standing around and we were all just hanging out talking. I looked up, and just as I did, Dan came walking over this little tiny hill that was more like a mound. I didn't know who he was, but I thought he was pretty cute. In Dan's story, this is the spot where he took that breath and fell in love with me, but I didn't know that at the time. He came over to our group and joined whatever conversation we were having. That was all. It's barely memorable, yet I remember it. Something happened in that moment that I didn't even realize.

We kept running into each other over the next couple of days. Now that I think back on it, he may have been stalking me. I wouldn't put it past him. One night at campfire, I sat by him and was cold, a common theme with me, so he gave me his blanket to keep me warm. I can still feel the butterflies in my stomach when I think about that moment. He wrapped it around me himself with chivalry like a prince would do for a princess. Then he told me to take it back to my cabin with me, in case it was cold there too. I never gave that blanket back. I still have it to this day. We ended up spending all of our free time together that week, hanging out on the sand dunes. Somewhere in our conversations I told him I had a boyfriend back home. He pretended that he didn't mind, that he just wanted to be friends. I think secretly he was waiting it out.

That's what we did. We were friends; we hung out all the time. As it turns out, not only did we attend the same high school and not know it, but we attended the same church youth group. How we could not know these things? Well, our high school was huge, and he was a whole grade ahead of me. My older sister knew Dan, but I didn't. Our youth group was also very large, around 80 kids crammed into one small basement.

I was new to the youth group at that time, so I didn't know very many people, but as friends, Dan gave me rides to youth group and rides home from school. He would seek me out in the hallways to see how my day was going. For almost a year we built up a healthy friendship, because I had that "other" boyfriend. I'm grateful for it; I think it is what made our relationship so strong.

One day, I finally came to my senses and realized that I wanted to be with Dan. That really, I had wanted to be with Dan since the first day I met him. So, I broke up with the other guy. I called Dan and cried to him about it. I fell asleep while on the phone, listening to his soothing voice telling me everything was going to be fine. I believed him.

Three weeks passed, and I was beginning to wonder if I had just been imagining that he liked me. Maybe he did just want to be friends. I found out later that one day he had a conversation with my best friend, Mari. (Mari has been my best friend since I was 12 years old. Mari was, is, and will always be my person, the one who will help me bury the body in the dead of night. Luckily, we haven't had a need for that yet, but she was great at helping me separate my dead husband's ashes. It takes a special person to do that with you.) I asked Mari to tell me the conversation that she and Dan had that day. She sheepishly grinned and said, "Uh, I don't remember that conversation." From what I can piece together, it went something like this:

Dan was waiting for me to be done with something and was standing around with Mari. She said, "So why aren't you her boyfriend yet?"

To which he stammered something akin to, "Umm, I'm not sure if she wants me to be."

Then Mari said, "Oh, she wants you to be. All you have to do is ask. So, hurry up already!"

That night Dan took me on our first actual date. Dan was a fierce nature lover, so we went to a nature conservatory in our town and walked along the trails. It was a gorgeous spring night. May 14, 1997 to be exact. I had just turned 17 in April. We held hands and talked, sat on a bench and looked at the pond. When I think back on it, I can still feel how my heart fluttered with anticipation. At the end of the trail we stopped. I don't remember his exact words, but it was beautiful and poetic because that's just how Dan talked. It was sort of like a proposal, and at the end of it he asked if he could be my boyfriend. I was standing on a small rock and he was on the ground, and we had our first kiss. It was true love's kiss. I could feel it and so could Dan; we just knew that this was something special. When we got back to his car, there was a rose waiting for me on the front seat.

From that moment on we were inseparable. The longest we were ever apart was three weeks in high school when Dan went on a mission trip to Romania. He came back from that trip and promised me he would never be apart from me that long again. He kept that promise until the day he died.

I've lost count of how many weeks we have been apart since he died, but it has been so much longer than three. I still count the months, though. As of this moment it has been three years and eight months since I have seen, touched, or talked to my soul mate.

Dan and I were both extremely involved in church youth group. We were what one could call core members of the youth group. We helped in church and Sunday school. Dan was even in charge of a 4th, 5th, and 6th grade youth group. We went on mission trips and were in "Disciples Club", a class after church for people that wanted to learn more about the Bible. That was us. As long as I've known Dan, all he ever wanted to do was show people that Jesus loved them. I liked that plan too, but I was much more into the history of the Bible. It was our thing that we did together.

Dan wrote about our youth group,

> ...the church was where I would meet my wife, find a sense of belonging, give my testimony, share in mission and feel my first sense of calling to the ministry. This is

where I first did the work of ministry, where I spoke into people's lives and had them speak into mine, where I acted as a shepherd for the people. Here I learned new and amazing truths about God, about myself, and about the existential questions that have always fascinated me.

Soon after we fell in love, Dan went on that three-week trip to Romania. It was the summer of 1997. Worried that I would miss him, he taped himself on a cassette talking to me. He told me stories, read me poems, and played me songs that reminded him of us. Every morning and evening I had a piece to listen to.

After he died, I had them converted to CDs so I could hear his voice again. I lie in my bed and laugh and cry and remember things I had forgotten. And try to fall asleep to the sound of his voice like I used to. They are beautiful and, in a way, they make me feel so close to him, like he could be lying next to me talking. But he's not. Just an 18-year-old recording.

I never considered myself beautiful, ever. Covered in red hair and freckles, I was teased mercilessly as a child. Then I met Dan. For whatever reason, he thought I was jaw droppingly beautiful. He told me I was beautiful every single day, more than once. He could go through every single physical feature and tell me why he loved it. Then he would go through every non-physical trait I had and tell me why he loved those. Once he made a list: "The Top 21 Things I Love to Like About Jennifer".

With Dan, I found confidence I didn't know I had. I began considering myself beautiful. I began believing I was as amazing as he said I was. I began believing I was magic. After all, Dan thought I was magic, so maybe I could be.

Dan was a year older than me, so he went off to Bible college while I stayed behind in Oregon to finish high school. He wanted to be a pastor/counselor, always both, never just one or the other. To him they went hand in hand. I had every intention of joining him there when I graduated, not because I was following him, but because I wanted to learn about what made this Bible thing tick. He called me every night and sometimes in the middle of the day. This was a big deal because we did not have cell phones, just old-fashioned landlines. I didn't even have an email account; we wrote letters back and forth and put them in the mail. I still have most of them. He came home almost every weekend just to see me. He drove 8 hours each way, which meant we basically only had one day together, but he said I was worth it. When the weather turned, he spent money he should have spent on books to fly home and see me. Finally, he said screw it. He couldn't stand being away from me any longer. He moved back home at the semester break, went to community college, and waited for me to finish high school. Then we went back to college together the next year.

When I got to college, everyone already knew who I was because Dan talked about me so much. It was a very small Christian college. I don't remember the exact student count, but I would say it was around 100 people total. Our youth group was bigger. The first day of college I walked up to the head resident of my dorm and introduced myself, with my parents right behind me. She said, "Oh yeah, Dan's fiancée. We've heard all about you." Well, actually, he hasn't asked me to marry him yet, and while I fully expect him to, you're freaking out my parents by calling me his fiancée.

The first weekend we were at school, Dan took me to get my first tattoo. A wooden cross on my ankle with a purple rose winding around it. He held my hand through the whole thing. He always said he knew we were meant to be together because our hands slipped together so easily, like they were made for each other.

On a beautiful fall day in October, Dan took me out on a date. I suspected this was it. I wanted to look extra special, so I borrowed my friend Katie's dress. It wasn't a fancy dress, just a dress he had never seen me in before. It was blue denim; simple, sweet. Dan took a picture of me in it. This was before the days of cameras on phones, so he had to use a real camera; it wasn't even digital, he had to get the film developed later. He said I just looked so beautiful he couldn't help it. Secretly, he wanted to have a photo of the night he asked me to marry him.

We went to a very fancy restaurant. I think it was the fanciest restaurant in Boise at the time. It was too fancy for our tastes, and we didn't love our dinner, but we laughed about it. We went for a walk at a nearby park. Dan had a small folder he said he wanted to show me. Inside was a poem he had written for us, about us, about our love. At the end of it, he knelt on one knee, which was exceedingly hard for him because he had just had knee surgery in August. He pulled out the most gorgeous ring I had ever seen in my life. He asked me to marry him as he put the ring on my finger. I didn't say anything! I thought the answer was obvious, plus I'm sure I was nodding my head. After a few seconds, Dan said, "Well, are you going to say yes?" I kissed him instead.

Throughout our dating and marriage, Dan was always writing me letters to tell me he loved me, to tell me he missed me, to tell me how his day was, or just because. Most were hand written; in the late nineties, typing was only for important things like school papers. If you were just scribbling love letters to your girlfriend, you still hand wrote them. He didn't sign a single one without telling me he loved me.

I love you so much. I love your eyes, I love your hair and I love your smile. I love that look you have when you're tired. I love the way you look at me when you're feeling all silly and try to tease me. I love the way you wipe your mouth off with your lips after I kiss you. I love that I can talk to you about anything and that I want to talk to you about everything. I love that I'm the first person you want to tell when happy and that I'm the first person you look for when you're sad. I love everything about you. I am never as happy as I am when I'm with you and I want to spend the rest of my life with you. I love you with everything that I am.

Ever since I was five years old, I have been in love with my mom's wedding dress and said I would wear it at my wedding. It was always going to be my dress. It came without a veil though; my mom didn't save that. And thank goodness she didn't, because while the dress was beautiful, the veil was dreadful. Mom's veil had a giant white silk lily that went right on the top of your head, and short white netting that puffed out from behind it. The first time I tried on my dress was at my future mother-in-law's house. It fit almost perfectly.

"Now I only need to buy a veil!" I said. My mother-in-law said she had her old veil in the closet and went to get it. I was trying to think of a way to get out of this predicament, assuming her veil would be hideous, like my mother's, when she came out with the most exquisite veil. It had very fine netting that was gathered with a clip at the top so you could place it anywhere. It was bordered with lace that matched the lace on my dress perfectly. It trailed all the way down my back and onto the floor. Truly, it is exactly what I would have picked out on my own. I got married to my Prince Charming in my mother's dress and my mother-in-law's veil. Dan, as usual, thought I looked stunning.

After the wedding we drove two hours to the beach. I was starving for the entire trip, because I was too busy smiling and talking at the reception to eat. We made it to the hotel where we were going to have our honeymoon, a gift from his parents. At one point during our stay, we went to the hotel lobby to rent a movie. The hotel clerk informed us that if we wanted to rent a movie, we would need to get our parents' permission. Dan informed him that our parents were not here because we were on our honeymoon.

Now I was married to my soulmate and best friend. We were going to live happily ever after, have four kids, buy a big house in the country, sit on the porch in rocking chairs, and hold hands while we watched our children and grandchildren play in the yard. Dan always said when we had had our 80th wedding anniversary, we could talk about whether or not we were ready to get a divorce.

We started to live our happily ever after. We worked, we played, we were madly in love. We dreamed of our children and our forever home. Our favorite pastime was looking through antique stores together, trying to find that one special treasure.

We started to read together every night and continued to do so throughout our marriage. We would almost always be reading the same series. Usually he would be a book ahead of me (so we each had a book) and he would ask what part I was on. When I would tell him, he would say something like, "Oh, yeah, just wait. It gets so much worse!" or "Haha! I know what's going to happen next!" Sometimes, we read a series together. We would lie in bed and I would have my head on his chest, and he would read the book aloud. I loved reading that way.

He would also tell me stories. Mostly stories about a magical land he made up, stories he wanted to turn into a series of chapter books for children. He tested them out on me. I would fall asleep listening to his voice. He never finished his stories. He died before he had time to write most of them down.

We did as much as we possibly could together because we wanted to be with each other. In 2006, we went on a dream trip to Israel. We both love history and it was totally amazing, incredible, and everything you might think the trip of a lifetime would be. When we got home, he asked me what my favorite part about the trip was. I said, "For three weeks, the only time we were ever apart was when one of us was in the bathroom." We got to spend every minute together: no jobs, no school, no commitments, and no errands. Just us. That was the best part of that trip.

"Yeah, that was my favorite part, too," he said.

We had our beautiful, perfect daughter in May of 2007. We loved our little family and were working on making it grow. We loved our little house and we loved our little neighborhood. I volunteered at India's school regularly and loved being a stay at home mom. Dan's job was going well, and he had just gotten a big promotion. Then it all changed. In an instant everything changed.

CHAPTER 3:

When My Time is Up,
Have I Done Enough?

∞ ∞ ∞

Note to self: breathe, just breathe.

Sometimes I wonder if Dan knew he was going to die early. He would talk about dying in weird cryptic ways. Sometimes he would straight up tell me he was going to die young. He would say that he hadn't accomplished enough with his life. I would say, "What are you talking about? We have tons of time! We have our whole lives ahead of us." I didn't take him seriously in the slightest. I rolled my eyes at him.

Dan always had this way about him. I don't really know how to describe it. He just knew stuff. I know that sounds weird and vague. I don't think that he knew he was going to die the day he did. But he would say things that now make me wonder.

He always said he was running out of time. When he turned 30, he said, "I'm already 30, I was supposed to have a book published by now. I'm running out of time." At 34 he said, "I should be on my third book!" I told him that writing books was something you did when you retired. Right now was the time for babies. He had years and years to write books. He didn't argue; he just said he was running out of time. He wanted to write about so many things: theology books, counseling books, parenting books, and marriage books. He wanted to write kids' chapter books and little kids' story books. He even wanted to write poetry books. I'm not much of a poetry person, but I loved his poetry. He had several pieces started, but he never got around to finishing even one book. He ran out of time, just like he said he was going to.

He wanted to do so many things. He wanted to get a master's in counseling, a master's in divinity, a doctorate in psychology, and a doctorate in divinity. Occasionally, he'd say something like, "And then I'll go back and get a doctorate in literature, just for fun." Because of finances, he didn't always get to take as many classes as he wanted to, which in his mind set him back. At the time of his death, he had gotten his master's in counseling and was two classes short of getting his master of divinity. Turns out, he ran out of time.

For four years we were in the process of adopting a baby. It was long and grueling and stressful. We wanted another baby so badly. While visiting friends in Idaho, the summer before he died, our social worker emailed us and said there was a mother considering us for adopting her babies; it happened that she was having triplets. We had gotten these emails a few times before, but I had a feeling that this was it. We were going to get these babies. This is what four years of waiting had been for, we were going to adopt the rest of our family, and then we wouldn't have to go through the awful adoption process again. I wasn't even scared at the prospect of having triplets; I knew Dan and I could handle it together. I prayed, and I prayed, and I prayed.

One day, Dan decided to go for a hike in the Boise foothills. It was several hours before he came back. That wasn't unusual, he loved getting lost on hikes. When we had some alone time, I asked him how his hike was, he said, "Well, I talked to God for a good long time."

I interrupted, "Yeah, are we getting our babies? We're getting our babies aren't we?"

He replied, "Jennifer, you're not going to like what I have to say. God told me that India had to be enough for us."

Guess what I did when my husband shared this profound revelation that he was taking seriously? I totally and completely blew him off. "Whatever, He did not, we're adopting a baby." He didn't say anything about it after that, and I know that he knew it bothered me. Instead, we thought up baby names for the rest of the weekend because that made me happy. We didn't get those triplets, we didn't get any baby. India had to be enough for us.

He was always worried about dying of a seizure. "You're being ridiculous," I would tell him. "People don't die of seizures, especially people who hardly ever have them." I was right, of course.

"No, Jennifer, these seizures are going to be the end of me." I didn't believe him; only .001% of people die of seizures, and Dan was not one of those people. Dan didn't even have enough seizures for us to say he had epilepsy. Yet he always told me he was worried his seizures would kill him. A month before he died, we had an appointment with a neurologist to check on his new medication. He asked her what the chances were of him dying from this. She said practically none. She said, "I can't legally say never because it happens, but it's so rare that I want to say never." She even flicked her wrist like she was pushing the thought away. I was relieved.

"See Dan? Even the seizure specialist neurologist said you don't die from seizures," I said. A month later Dan died of a seizure, he was the .001%, and somewhere in his head, he knew that.

At the same time, he wanted to live to be over 100. He told me he would love me his whole life and then some. That I believed. I had no doubt it was true. Looking back, I think he told me these things because it's truly what he wanted to happen. He was a dreamer and he had grand dreams, but he also had a sense that his dreams wouldn't come to be.

I wish I had listened to him. I wish I hadn't taken our life for granted. I wish I hadn't taken our future for granted. I thought we had all the time in the world. We were supposed to. I wish I had encouraged him to write his books instead of telling him he would have time later. If we had known, truly known that we didn't have all the time in the world, I like to think we would have done something super romantic like run away to Europe and see all the castles, or something else that was on our someday list. I like to think that we would have treasured every single second the three of us spent together. I like to think he would have imparted all his wisdom to India and me. He would have told us how to be brave and strong without him. He would have told me what to do. He could have told us at least a million more times that he loved us. We could have said goodbye.

> *If today the mountains crumbled*
> *And fell into the sea*
> *And the breath of life God gave*
> *Was taken back from me*
>
> *If all the world was ending*
> *And there was nothing I could do*
> *Do you know that my last thoughts*
> *Would certainly be of you*
>
> *And don't you know if time would stop*
> *It would not be a pain to me*
> *If my last vision upon this earth*

Was your face that I would see

For in your eyes I saw
A world that was so at peace
And that thought would be on my heart
If today all things would cease

If today's the day I meet
The only God above
I'll be certain to speak of you
And how I fell in love.

Dan wrote me that poem while we were dating in high school, 20 years ago. He also started having seizures in high school. No one can say with certainty why he started having the seizures, but we suspect it was from being knocked around in his years on the wrestling team. The seizures were never really a problem. They were completely controlled by medication. We never even called it epilepsy. When it came up, which was rare, I would say, "Well, he sort of has a seizure condition, but not really. He has one every few years, and that's it." Most of our family didn't even know about it, because it wasn't a big deal. He took his medication every day and he was fine.

I remember when he first told me about his seizures. It was also the first time he had one, in spring of 1997. We hadn't been dating that long, a month maybe. I was in the kitchen of my parents' house and he came over to visit. He stood just inside the doorway and I had my back turned to him just talking away. I turned around and looked into his beautiful bright blue eyes. All around his eyes were bright red dots, like little pin pricks, especially under his eyes.

"What happened to your face?" I said, astonished. He didn't answer. I thought perhaps he had gotten in a fight or something, and I asked him again. Tears welled up in his eyes as he told me he had had a seizure. He wasn't crying because he feared the seizures, he was crying because he was afraid I would break up with him. Idiot. Didn't he know I was already in love with him? There was no turning back. The red dots were capillaries that had burst during the seizure. We talked for a while, and I honestly don't remember what we said, it was so long ago. When he left my mind was at ease. I wasn't worried about it. He had to have a few tests and the doctor would give him some medication, and everything would be fine. I went with him to those tests. They put little electrodes all over his head and monitored his brain function while we held hands.

Shortly after that we went on a trip to Boise to visit the college where Dan was going to go in the fall. Dan was driving, and he started to stare off into space. I asked him if he was OK, and he didn't answer. He pulled off to the side of the road, pulled the brake, and just sat there staring at nothing. This was the first seizure I ever witnessed. It was so small I didn't even know it was a seizure for sure. It was not like in the movies. Just a few small twitches and then he came back to life. I asked him what happened, and he said that was a seizure. I insisted that I drive the rest of the way and he begrudgingly let me. He was fine for the rest of the weekend. It was years and years before he had another one. We got married in 1999 and by the time I graduated college in 2003, he still hadn't had a single seizure.

The next one he had was in 2005. He was working, going to grad school, and doing his internship. It had been so long since he had had a seizure that he and the doctor decided to try reducing the dosage on his medication. One night we were sleeping, and I woke up to the bed shaking. He was having a seizure, I was certain, and this one looked like it did in the movies. Jerking. Shaking. Unconscious. I was terrified. During the seizure he bit his tongue badly and it was bleeding everywhere. Still, it was very short, less than a minute. I was so scared and didn't know what to do. He had rolled over and started snoring. I pushed on his shoulder and tried to get his attention, "Dan, wake up. Dan!" he grunted, shoved my hand away and continued to snore loudly. He seemed more or less alright, but I still felt like I should do something, so I called his parents. His dad answered the phone.

I said, "Dan had a seizure and I don't know what to do!"

His dad asked, "Do you want us to come over there?"

"Yes," I answered, and they were on their way. I think most young married couples tend to sleep without clothes. This would never do! His parents were coming over. I tried to wake Dan, but he kept snoring. I tried to put some pants on him myself, but he jerked away from my touch and kicked his leg up. It hit me smack in the chest and I went flying off the bed, just like on TV. Later, it was very comical, but I was not amused at the time. When his parents got there, ten minutes later, Dan was awake but groggy.

"Why did you call my parents? I'm perfectly fine. You didn't have to call and wake them up. I'm fine."

Indeed, except for his bleeding tongue, he seemed fine. His parents went home after ten minutes, satisfied that everything was okay. The next morning his mom brought us milkshakes for breakfast, and Dan, again, told us he was fine and that everybody had gotten worked up over nothing. He talked to his doctor and went up to his regular medication dosage.

Several more years passed. Nearly a decade passed, in fact. We had a baby in 2007, and she was seven years old before he had another seizure.

The Sunday before Thanksgiving 2014 we were asleep, and I woke up to the bed shaking. Dan was having a seizure, making small, jerky, unconscious movements. It was so short that by the time I turned the light on and sat up, it was over. I suppose I took his C-Pap machine off, but I don't remember doing that. He rolled over and started snoring. I shook his arm and he tried to shove me away. I tried to get his attention by saying his name.

"Dan, wake up baby. You had a seizure. Dan." He grunted, but he was clearly sleeping, snoring loudly. I laid there for an hour or two and worried about him. He probably shouldn't go to work tomorrow so he can rest, I thought. He should probably call the doctor and make an appointment to make sure everything's okay. Then I fell asleep too.

Monday morning, I woke up to the sound of the shower going and the smell of steam coming from the bathroom. This is how I usually woke up. Dan would get up before me and shower. I walked into the bathroom.

"Good morning babe, did you sleep well?" he asked. I opened the shower door and just stared at him.

"What?" he said.

"Uh, do you remember that you had a seizure last night?" I asked.

"No I didn't."

"Yes, you did."

"Nuh uh, you're lying," he tried to tease me.

"Yes, you did Dan, I was there. I think you should stay home today and rest."

"Can't stay home, I got to go to work. I feel fine."

"Don't you think you should call the doctor?" I insisted.

"Jennifer, it was a fluke, I'm fine." And off he went to work. I kind of thought it was a fluke too. It had been so long since he had one, it must have been a fluke.

Because it was Thanksgiving break, we had family in town. All the ladies in his family were going out to our traditional nice dinner and the kids and dads were going out to a more kid friendly restaurant. The timing meant that I wouldn't see Dan between his getting home from work and me going to dinner. I texted him at 5:00 that evening.

"How was work? How are you feeling? Did you call the doctor?" He didn't respond, which was typical of him, so I didn't worry. In the middle of dinner, I got a text from him. It was very cryptic. I hate cryptic texts. It said, "Oops, I did it again." He was trying to be funny. I texted back.

"Did what? Had another seizure? Are you okay? Are you at your dad's house? What's going on? Do you need me to come home?" Now I was starting to worry. I wasn't sure if he actually did have another seizure, or if he was talking about something else entirely.

Don't send cryptic texts. Just don't.

I was with his mother and sisters in law, and I didn't want to worry them, so I kept eating and texting him. Finally, I got out of him that he had a small seizure while eating dinner at the restaurant with his dad, brother, brother's kids, and India.

"Oh yeah, and one today at work too," he texts, as an afterthought, as if it's no big deal.

"Ok we're on our way home. India can spend the night with Grandpa and Grandma, and we can go to urgent care." He hemmed and hawed about whether he actually needed to go, but I insisted. Still not wanting to worry his mother, I waited until we got in the driveway of their house and then blurted out, "So, Dan's had three seizures since last night. I'm going to take him to urgent care and India is going to spend the night here. OK, thanks." And with that, I jumped out of the car. I think at least two of his sisters in law had absolutely no idea what I was talking about. Dan hadn't had a seizure since they married into the family.

I went inside, Dan was sitting in the recliner playing on his phone. India was playing in the living room with her cousins. I took a minute to pull India aside, and asked her if she was okay, and if she was scared when Daddy got kind of sick at the restaurant. She shrugged it off and wanted to go play with her cousins. I thought maybe it was small enough that she didn't really notice. It seemed not to bother her, so I didn't worry about it. I went back to Dan and said, "Okay. Let's go." He looked at me, annoyed that I was making him go, but he didn't argue. Dan and I got in the car and I said, "Urgent care, here we come!"

"No, Jennifer, do not go to urgent care. We have to go straight to the ER." My heart started racing. Was he about to have another one?

"Urgent care is closed for the night," he laughed. He was trying to make light of the situation for me, he wasn't worried at all. He was more annoyed that everyone else was so worried about him.

When we got to the ER, Dan told them what was going on and they immediately made him sit in a wheelchair. Even I thought that was ridiculous. It's not like he was having a seizure that second. He had to describe his seizures for the nurse. From the way he described the one at work, and the one at the restaurant, they were comparable to the size of the one he had while sleeping the night before, if not smaller. They were no big deal, minimal, they only lasted a few seconds. It's not like they were huge giant seizures. Not like on TV; they always exaggerate on TV. They put him in a bed for observation. He was annoyed; he wanted to go home and sleep. None of this was necessary, he kept saying, he was fine. He needed to go to the bathroom, and he was irritated that they wouldn't let him go without a nurse.

"Really guys, you are all overreacting. I'm fine," he tried to convince them.

"Ha, now you know how I felt when I was having India and they wouldn't let me go to the bathroom alone," I teased.

The doctor decided that he was having seizures because the medication he had been on for the last 17 years was absorbing too fast. They decided to change his medication. It was the only thing to do. Before they got the new medication in his system, he had another seizure. This was by far the biggest and worst seizure I had ever seen him have. It came right out of a medical drama, like ER or Grey's Anatomy. I guess TV does get it right sometimes. Big, jerky movements. Legs kicking, arms flying, hospital bed shaking. Doctors were calling out medications to give him and ordering people around. I was sitting in a chair in the corner, crying silently and trying to stay out of the way. It felt like it lasted forever. I was terrified. There were doctors and nurses surrounding him, helping him, and I was still terrified. Then he rolled over and went to sleep, snoring loudly. I remember thinking, "Thank God we were already at the hospital, I would have had to call 911 for that one." I texted his mom to tell her what had just happened, and that we would indeed be spending the night in the hospital.

They got his new medication in him and made him spend the night for observation. He didn't have any more seizures. A groggy Dan kept trying to convince the nurses to let him go home. He even tried to hire one. I had to explain to her that it was alright; he ran a mental health facility and he was always looking for good nurses. I stayed with him, sleeping in a chair. Dan tried to convince me to go home and get some sleep, he was fine, and I wouldn't get any rest in that chair. He did have nerve, but seeing as he had just had a giant seizure and was on tons of medication, I won that one. I slept with my shoes on, in jeans and a sweatshirt. They were not the most comfortable clothes, and it was not the most comfortable chair, but I was fine. It was just for one night, this was by far the worst of it, and I hoped that with his new medication he would have seizures even more rarely. So, basically never.

The next morning, he took a selfie in the hospital bed, hooked up to all the monitors. He sent it to a preteen girl we know who has epilepsy, so that she would know she wasn't alone. Her mom texted me back, "Are you guys alright? What happened?" I told her the story.

"We are fine, really, don't worry about us, we are checking out now. It's Thanksgiving, so he has the rest of the week off work to rest." That was the truth. That's how unworried about it we both were. We went home and snuggled on the couch all day and watched TV. We were excited that India was still with Dan's parents, so we could watch grownup TV. "It's like we're on a date!" we teased.

The next day I took India to a friend's house for a play date so Dan could have another day to rest. He cleaned the house for me instead. He was a little sluggish and tired the rest of the week, but he was fine. He was totally fine for the next six weeks.

> *I have prayed for God to intervene with a miracle in my life. In reality I pray for little miracles everyday about all kinds of things, everything from "please get my car to start" to "please give me the motivation and energy to get this paper done". I have prayed for big obvious miracles too. I have prayed that God would heal my various injuries from wrestling for nine years. I have prayed that if He will not do that to at least keep me functioning and able bodied for the rest of my marriage. I trust God in these things. I have seen Him work miracles before and I know that He wants what is best for me and that He wants to use me. If He needs me in this condition to serve Him then I will stay this way. If he needs me in a different condition, then He will change me.*
>
> *— Dan*

CHAPTER 4:

The World Turned Upside Down

∞ ∞ ∞

This is not going to be pretty. We're talking violence,
strong language, adult content.
— Buffy the Vampire Slayer

It's about to get deep. I'm about to tell the story of Dan dying. It's not a pleasant story; he didn't drift off quietly in his sleep at a ripe old age. He didn't finally get to rest after a long struggle with cancer or some other vicious disease. He wasn't murdered. He wasn't in a car accident. He just died. He just died while I stood there and watched. For me, it was the most traumatic thing that has ever happened. I can remember every single thing about him dying. All of it. I watched my husband die. I just stood there terrified, so terrified that I froze. I have never felt such fear. So terrified that I couldn't remember how to do CPR (I'd been trained years ago). Maybe that would have saved him, but I didn't do it. I couldn't do it. I was too scared. Maybe it wouldn't have done anything; maybe it was already too late. I just don't know.

It was really an uneventful day as far as last days go. There was nothing special or spectacular about it. We went to church. Dan did India's hair that morning in six long braids. He did her hair regularly; he had me teach him how to braid just so he could braid India's hair. He almost always brushed her hair; she liked it better when he did it. She said he didn't pull as hard. At church, she was asked who made her hair so pretty and she very shyly said, "My Daddy did it." I think everyone was expecting her to say Mommy, but it wasn't my doing. It was Dan's.

The Crystal Ballroom, in downtown Portland, was having a big 100th birthday celebration and my siblings convinced us to go. It was crowded and loud, and we didn't stay long. Instead, we went to one of those chocolate drinking places, where they give you a baby cup full of melted chocolate and expect you to sip it gently rather than downing it in one gulp. We had never done that before and Dan loved it. He posted on Facebook that it tasted like heaven. He was a chocoholic.

We went to Powell's bookstore and bought India a Dr. Seuss book. India has had me read that book to her a few times. I always do it, trying not to make my voice quiver and trying not to cry. I remember that book as the last thing he got for her, the last thing we got her together. A silly Dr. Seuss book called *Because a Little Bug Went Ka-Choo!* I don't know if she remembers it that way, or if she realizes it's the last thing Daddy bought her on the last day Daddy was alive. Maybe she does, and maybe that's why we've only read it a few times. After Powell's, we went and got a cheeseburger. The tiny restaurant was so crowded that I sat on a stool with India on my lap and Dan had to stand up. I remember him rolling his eyes at me, annoyed at the situation. Dan carried India around about half the day because she was tired of walking.

"My legs are little," she said to convince him to carry her, not that she had to try hard. He just swooped her up and off they went, adventuring. Finally, we headed home. There was traffic, even on a Sunday. Portland is getting really crowded these days. Dan probably commented on wanting to move further out to the country. It was around 4:00 or 5:00 PM.

Then my memory blacks out. I just can't remember what happened after that, until around 11PM when it all started. It's very strange to me. One would think if I blacked anything out, it would be Dan dying, but nope. I remember that. I think maybe it was simply so boring and typical that there was no reason for me to remember it. I believe we watched TV and ate dinner; that's what we typically did. I don't remember cooking dinner or what we ate. maybe Dan cooked dinner that night, I don't know.

We put India to bed. We had the same bedtime routine every night. First, we would all snuggle in our bed. Dan would read a chapter or two of whatever book we were on. Then we would take India into her room and tuck her into bed. We would say our prayers and then sing The Daddy Mommy Song. We would each sing our respective parts and then we would say together, "It just makes your heart so big!" Sometimes India would join in in the last line, her little voice full of love. Then Dan would tell her one of his stories he had made up just for her. He wanted to turn them into a book someday. It always ended with us each giving her a kiss and telling her we loved her more than anything. Dan would always go last and as he walked out the door, he would say, "I'll see you in the morning." This was our nightly routine; it wouldn't have been any different even if I could remember.

Dan and I probably watched some more TV, what we would call "grown up TV". Stuff you can't watch with a seven-year-old in the room, like The Walking Dead or Criminal Minds. Both shows were favorites of ours, both shows I haven't watched since. Then we went to bed.

I don't remember the last conversation I had with Dan. I don't remember the last time he kissed me or the last thing he said to me. He generally said something like, "Goodnight, I love you," as he leaned over and gave me a kiss. In all likelihood, that's what happened, but I don't remember. I can't remember the last time he said he loved me or the last time he kissed me. His parents were picking him up at 6:00 AM the next day to take him to the airport for a business trip so that I didn't have to wake India up to take him myself. He would kiss me goodbye before he left. He always did. He would probably need me to braid his hair, and I would sit up and do it, still half asleep.

"Go back to bed, Love," he would say as he left the room.

We went to bed at 11. I was asleep for maybe ten minutes when the bed started shaking. His C-PAP machine was making a weird gurgling noise, like he was choking or breathing funny. I jumped up and ripped the C-PAP mask off of his face. Dan was having a seizure; his body was shaking uncontrollably.

And then it was over. It was short. Not more than 30 seconds. It was small, not anywhere near as big as the one he had in the hospital at Thanksgiving or even the one he had ten years before where he almost bit off a piece of his tongue. It was similar to the one he had in bed the week before Thanksgiving, the one that started this series, the one we both wrote off as a "fluke". It was a small seizure.

In those 30 seconds I thought, "Oh man, we are going to have a big fight in the morning. He's supposed to go to California for work. I don't think he should go now, but he's going to want to go anyway."

I can hear him now, "I'm fine, Jennifer. Stop worrying, everything's fine." He always said that.

Then everything changed. Something was wrong. In any of his other seizures I'd seen him have, he wasn't "all there" afterward. He was pretty out of it, like waking up from anesthesia. I might get a mumble as he rolled over and went back to sleep. Usually, I would try to get his attention by nudging him in the shoulder. "Dan, wake up. Dan, you had a seizure. Dan, can you hear me?" He would throw his hand up, shove me away, make an unintelligible grumble, and continue to snore. That was how he always responded. Then, I would lay awake for hours worrying about him.

Not this time. This time he didn't move. I pushed on his shoulder. He didn't move. I started talking to him. "Dan. Dan. Wake up. Dan. Dan. Dan, can you hear me? Wake up!" He didn't do anything. He didn't move at all, not even an inch. I was starting to get really scared. I pulled open his eyelid and his eye had rolled up in his head. I put my ear on his chest. His heart was beating extremely fast. Or was it mine? Or both? I couldn't tell. I didn't know what to do.

I ran out to the living room and grabbed my phone off the brown dresser where it always was at night; we didn't bring cell phones to bed. I dialed 911. I have never in my life dialed 911. I ran back to Dan, still in our bed, and looked at the clock. It said 11:15. At 11:15 I called 911; I will never forget. There was a voice prompt on the phone that said something like, "Say help if you need help."

I said, "Help! Help! I need help!" As I was doing this, I was thinking, "Dan is going to be so mad at me in the morning. He's going to say 'Why did you bother calling them, Jennifer? I was fine. They have people that really need help; they don't need to waste their time with me. I'm fine."

A lady answered the phone and asked me what the emergency was. I told her that my husband had a seizure and he wasn't responding to me. I needed help; I didn't know what to do.

"No, he has a seizure condition, but something is wrong. Help!" She asked me if he was breathing. I looked at him closely, but I couldn't tell if he was breathing. She asked me if I could hear his heartbeat. I put my ear to his chest and I couldn't tell. Several times I put my ear to his chest and lifted it back up. I thought I heard a heartbeat, then I didn't, then I thought I heard it again. I was crying, and I kept saying "Dan! Dan!" over and over again. Remembering back, sometimes it feels like I was talking in a whisper and sometimes it feels like I was screaming at the top of my lungs. I don't know which one it actually was.

She asked me where he was and I said in the bed. She asked me if I thought I could move him down to the floor. "I don't know, I can try I guess." So, I pulled on him. I grabbed his ankles and pulled hard on his legs. He fell to the floor with a loud thump. I gasped at the loudness of it, but he didn't move on his own at all. He didn't shake his head and say, "Ow, what'd you pull me off the bed for?" He didn't do anything. He just laid there. She told me to lift his neck up to help him breathe. I tried, but it was hard to move him, and I didn't want to hurt him. I don't know if I did it right. Was that enough, or too much? I put my head on his chest again. I still couldn't tell if I heard his heart beating.

"Dan, Dan! Wake up, Dan!" I was crying so hard. She asked me if I knew CPR. I couldn't remember. I had taken the class when India was a baby, but I couldn't remember how. I didn't think I would ever really need to do it. After all, if I were ever in a situation like that, Dan would be with me and he was highly trained in it.

I ran to the front door to open it for the paramedics. I saw the fire truck with lights pull up to our house and waved them inside. I don't know how many were there, but it felt like a lot. Two of them followed me back to the bedroom. They got on either end of Dan. One of them kind of shrugged at the other one. I don't know why. Was it a "he's already dead" shrug? I've always wondered. They picked him up, one at the legs and the other one under the arms, and carried him out to the living room. They laid him on his back right in the walkway of the living room and the kitchen, arms out, spread eagle. Now, when someone uses that phrase, I always picture Dan in that position. One foot was touching the wood floor of the dining room.

I stood in the opening of the hallway; I couldn't see his face, because paramedics were in my way. I could just see his feet and a little bit of his legs. 911 was still on my phone, so I picked up Dan's phone and called my sister Melinda. I called Melinda for one reason and one reason only: Dan and I were going to go to the hospital, and somebody had to stay with India. Melinda lived three minutes away. Melinda would be here in three minutes. No answer. I called again. Melinda answered the phone and I screamed at her, "YOU HAVE TO COME OVER RIGHT NOW! RIGHT NOW, MELINDA! YOU HAVE TO COME OVER RIGHT NOW!" I don't think she recognized Dan's phone number because she wasn't sure that it was me. She said in a questioning voice, "Jenny?" Or maybe I was just screaming and crying too hard for her to understand me. I screamed again, "YOU HAVE TO COME OVER RIGHT NOW!" I guess she said OK or something? I guess I put the phone down? It wasn't in my hand anymore.

The paramedics were working on Dan, but I couldn't see what they were doing. Someone was standing in my way. I was crying so hard I couldn't really see anything. Someone asked me if anyone else was in the house.

"My daughter...she's sleeping...she's seven." A paramedic led me into our library and she sat me in the rocking chair. I sat there curled up in a ball, rocking, crying, and praying out loud, "Please God, please God, please fix Dan. Please God, Please God, please fix Dan." It's all I could think of to say. It felt like I did that for hours.

I heard the screen door open and Melinda's voice say slowly and drawn out, "What happened?" Then she was on top of me, holding me, her hair in my face. Melinda was there, I wasn't alone anymore. I kept praying for God to fix Dan. At some point, a paramedic said I needed to call Dan's parents. I said, "I can't. I can't call them." So Melinda did it.

She said, "Dan had a seizure you need to come up here...They're here." I guess she was talking about the paramedics.

The paramedic said that Dan's heart was not beating well. I said, "But it's still beating?" She said NO, it wasn't beating "good enough". I was confused. What does "not beating good enough" even mean? A beating heart is a beating heart, isn't it? If your heart is beating, you are alive. If it's not, you're not alive. It's pretty simple, I thought. No, it wasn't simple. Dan's heart was "not beating good enough". They were going to try one more thing to help Dan, but they didn't think it would work. I guess they were on the phone with a doctor from the hospital. Someone told me that afterward.

Melinda asked if we were going to the hospital, and the paramedic said NO. We weren't going to the hospital. That was it. I don't remember anyone actually telling me that Dan had died. I don't know that they did. That's how I knew he was gone. We wouldn't be going to the hospital. We wouldn't be going anywhere. Dan was dead.

The paramedic asked me if I wanted to see him. I didn't know if I did, but I got up anyway. My whole body was shaking, and I was crying so hard I couldn't see. We walked through the kitchen. I kept saying, "This isn't my life. This isn't what happens to me," over and over and over again. We got to the doorway of the kitchen and the dining room. I froze. I could see Dan out of the corner of my eye. His arms were spread straight out, his legs were together, and there was a white sheet covering him up to his chest. I couldn't move anymore. The paramedics tucked Dan's arms to his sides under the sheet. It wasn't one of our sheets. It didn't come from our house. It was a white sheet, a hospital sheet. It had a blue tint to it. I didn't move. He didn't have any tubes or machines or anything like that on him. I guess they moved them all away for me.

Standing in the doorway of my kitchen and dining room, I was between two worlds: one where Dan was alive and one where he wasn't. I didn't do anything. I was frozen to that spot. My feet wouldn't move. The paramedic said I should sit down so I did. I slid down the wall and sat on the floor in the doorway. I just kept saying, "This isn't my life. This isn't what happens to me." I could see Dan out of the corner of my eye. He was gone. The whole thing felt like it took hours and hours. I remember looking at the clock when I called 911, and it was 11:15 PM. Later, when I looked at Dan's death certificate, his time of death is 12:01 AM. 46 minutes.

I never touched Dan again. I didn't hold his hand. I didn't kiss his forehead. I didn't lay my head on his chest. Not even at the funeral viewing did I touch him again. I couldn't. My brain knew he was dead, but if I touched him, that would make it real. I didn't want it to be real.

I was back into our library. I don't remember moving, but there we were. I called my dad. I told him the same thing I told Melinda. "You have to come over here right now. Right now." He only lived three minutes away too. My dad came stumbling into the library (he always trips over his giant feet) and immediately put his arms around me, so tight it hurt. We stayed that way for a long time. Melinda was there. Melinda called one of my best friends, Mari. She lived four hours away in Seattle, but she was coming. She was coming. Dan's parents and his brother Jerry showed up. They came in the front door; they had to walk past Dan. I don't know if someone told them Dan was dead on the living room floor before they saw him or not. I hope so. I wish I had thought to have everyone come through the garage, so they didn't have to walk past Dan. My other sister Pauline came over. I heard someone throwing up outside. Was it her? I don't know. I heard a guttural scream of agony from outside. I think it might have been Dan's brother Jerry. His parents were sitting in chairs someone had brought in from the dining room. Just sitting. His mom had tears streaming down her face. His dad just had an empty stare. I was sitting on the couch with my head buried in my dad's shoulder. I think my sisters were on the other side of me.

Someone said I should call the pastor at our church. I didn't have his number, and I didn't want to call him anyway. I knew who I wanted to call from church. Another young widow, except that was 40 years ago. Her daughter was a year old when her daddy died. Now she is all grown up, and our daughters are best friends. She would know what to do; I was sure she would know what to do; she would tell me what to do. I called her.

"Pat Smith? This is Jenny Stults...Dan died." Was I screaming, or crying, or both?

She answered back in complete shock, "Dan died? What do you mean Dan died?"

"He had a seizure and he died. He died. I called you because you know." As in "you have done this before, you know what to do".

"Yes. Yes, I know." I don't remember how that conversation ended, I knew she would let our church know.

At some point I realized that India was still asleep. India had slept through the entire thing. How was that possible? We were so loud! Maybe she was awake and just too scared to come out of her room? Oh God, what if she heard the whole thing? No, no. She would have called for me. She must have slept through it. To this day I don't know which it is. Only once ever has she alluded to anything about the night Dan died. This was the entire conversation:

"Mommy, did you know that the night Daddy died, I woke up? I knew that he had died."

"How did you know Daddy had died?"

"I just knew. I predicted it. Like when you sat in the chair with me to tell me the cat died. I knew that's what you were gonna tell me. Plus, I heard noises."

"Noises like what? Like the workers (paramedics) talking, or other noises?"

"Like the workers talking. One of them sounded like Uncle Dave."

I like to tell myself that by the grace of God, India slept through the whole thing. That she doesn't remember because she was asleep. Other times, I say I am deluding myself because I want to make myself feel better. Of course she was awake. How could she have possibly stayed asleep through all that commotion? She's just too scared to talk about it. Then I think, no, if she were awake, I would have known. She would have called for me; she would have come out of her room; she would have done something. I would have known. I can't bear the thought of her awake, all alone and afraid in her room listening to Mommy screaming and paramedics making noise, and not hearing Daddy's calm reassuring voice.

I sent Melinda to go and check on her. I had no idea what she would find, my baby sleeping soundly or sitting up in bed, too terrified to move. Melinda didn't come back and didn't come back. Then I started to panic about India, so I went into her room too. They were both awake, lying in her loft bed. Melinda thinks India woke up when she came in to check on her.

I told India in as happy a voice as I could muster, which probably wasn't the slightest bit convincing, "Grandma and Grandpa are in the library waiting for us, so let's go see them!" I had a problem though. To get there I had to walk right past Dan, and I could not let India see that. I told her we were going to be sneaky and play a game. I picked her up and I put the pirate blankie that Dan and I had gotten her for her third birthday over her head. That was her blankie and she took it everywhere. I said, "No peeking, and no matter what, you have to stay under the blankie until I say you can come out!" She put her head down on my shoulder, and we walked down the hall, past her Daddy's body lying on the living room floor, through the kitchen, and into the library.

I sat down on the couch with her on my lap. I said I had to tell her something. I had no idea what to say, but this is what came out of my mouth: "Sometimes people die because they are really, really old like Great Grandpa Leo. Sometimes people die because they are really, really sick. Sometimes people die, and no one knows why, and that's what happened to Daddy. Daddy died and he is living in heaven now." One tear came out of her left eye, and she whipped it away. She didn't say anything, she didn't cry, she didn't ask any questions, she just sat on my lap. I guess everyone else started talking, or maybe we just sat there in silence. I don't remember.

At some point India said she needed to go potty. "Ok let's go," I told her. As I stood up, I remembered that to get to the bathroom we would have to walk past Dan's body again. So, we played the hide under the blankie game to and from the bathroom. She didn't ask any questions.

We all sat in the library. Talking. Waiting. For what, I'm not sure. A chaplain? A social worker? The funeral home? All of them? We were waiting. Somebody said something about Saturday. I looked at my dad; I had been meaning to ask him this question for days.

"Hey, you want to come over early on Saturday and help me put up the decorations for Pat and Al's party?" Pat and Al are Dan's parents. Saturday was their 40th wedding anniversary; we had been planning the party for months. Family was flying in from across the country. Dan was going to be the MC. He had started working on his speech; he wasn't going to procrastinate this time.

Pat looked at me and said, "I don't think we're going to have a party anymore." What was she talking about, not having a party?

"What! Why not?" I asked her, like she had suddenly gotten up and decided she didn't want to have her big party anymore. What was her problem anyway?

She replied, "Well I think we're going to have a funeral instead, Honey." Oh, right. Dan's dead. We need to have a funeral. I guess that's what you call shock.

"Oh," I said. "Do we have to do it so soon?" His mom was being so practical.

"Well, everyone will already be here. They all have plane tickets already." Oh, right. So I guess we're having a funeral on Saturday instead of an anniversary party.

The chaplain was there. I'm not really sure what he was supposed to be doing. He noticed our wedding pictures on the wall. He recognized the minister that married us. They were friends. Small world.

A social worker came. He said he needed to ask me some questions; I didn't want to answer questions about Dan dying in front of India. I sat her on Auntie's lap and told her I would be right back. She started to cry a little; she didn't want me to leave her. I walked past Dan again. Every time I try not to look at his face, just his feet. We went into the bedroom that was a nursery for our future child. All the social worker wanted was information, like our names and address. He gave me a packet about kids and grief. We could have done all that with India. We could have done all that without me walking past Dan again. Anybody could have answered those questions, I didn't even have to do it. Someone else could have done it for me. I went back into the library with everyone else.

The funeral home came to take Dan away. I didn't have a funeral home picked out, so they just called one. I guess that's a thing, to have your funeral home pre-picked out. Just not when you're 36. Dan and I had never discussed which funeral home we preferred. In adult code, they told us they were taking Dan away and if anyone wanted to see him before they did so, now was the time. I think maybe some other people went out there. Pat. Al. Jerry. I didn't go. I didn't want to see him like that anymore. I didn't want to see him like that ever, but I guess that didn't happen. I didn't want to leave India again. I didn't want to explain to her where I was going. I didn't want her to know her Daddy had been lying dead in the living room this whole time. The people from the funeral home came and told me they were all done and leaving. I could let India in the living room now; we could go to sleep now.

Sleep? Ha! Like we were really going to sleep. We tried anyway; we didn't know what else to do. What were we supposed to do? I sent Melinda into my room to change the sheets on the bed. I don't know why; they weren't dirty. It just seemed strange to go back into the same bed where Dan started to die. When she was done, I carried India into our room and laid her in the middle of the bed. Then I crawled in and Melinda crawled into Dan's spot. She tried to make it okay. "Yay, Auntie gets to sleep with you too!" We didn't sleep, any of us. We just laid there. My dad and my other sister Pauline slept in the living room, or rather laid in the living room pretending to sleep.

I couldn't bring myself to call my three besties: Stacie, Jacque, and Shirley. So, I wrote them a message in our group chat instead. The group chat we had had going for years now. The one where we complain about our husbands and kids together. The one where we laughed and prayed together. The one where we talked every day.

"I'm sorry, I know I should call you, but I just can't. Dan had a seizure, I called 911, they came but it was too late, they couldn't save him. He died. Dan died." I wrote that message somewhere around 3:00 AM, knowing it would be the first thing they saw when they woke up. Man, that was really shitty of me.

You would think that I would want to forget this. That I would want to forget everything about that awful night. Where, in less than one hour, I went from having a completely healthy husband to being a widow. And a huge part of me does. But another part of me feels like I have to remember. Like it is my duty, as the only one who was there, to witness it. Sadly, it is part of his story and part of mine. I feel like I would be doing him a disservice to forget how he died. So, as much as I want to forget it, I can't. Even if I was able to, I can't. Maybe that's why I'm writing the book, so I never forget.

CHAPTER 5:

Will they tell my story?

∞ ∞ ∞

I think I slept for an hour, if that. I got out of bed somewhere around 5:00 or 6:00 AM. It was Monday, January 12, 2015. I went out to the dining room and started clearing off the table. It was covered in stuff: mail, India's backpack, papers Dan brought home from work. You know, that's what a dining table is used for. This action woke up my two sisters; they asked me what I was doing.

"Clearing off the table. People will be coming over with food. We will need somewhere to put it." My family is Catholic; it's what they do. That thought was very rational of me.

The next thing I remember is exactly that: people coming over. Certainly, it wasn't 6:00 AM anymore, but I don't recall the time passing. That day is all a rushed blur. I remember snippets, but they are not necessarily in chronological order.

India was awake and unwilling to leave my side for anything, not even the bathroom. Little did I know that it would be more than a year before she was. To distract her, I asked her to go outside and feed the animals. She would only go if I went too. So that's what we did. Dan had been dead roughly eight hours and we were feeding the chickens and the bunnies.

While outside, Dan's brother Gregg and his wife Dina arrived. She came outside to find me. I remember her walking across the yard toward me. My older sister Desi had magically appeared and made breakfast. My house smelled of bacon, eggs, and hash browns. And Dan was dead. One of his favorite meals and he wasn't going to eat it ever again. I didn't feel like eating, but I tried to get India to eat something. She refused. Two of my besties, Stacie and Jacque, had shown up. Jacque's husband handed me coffee from our favorite coffee shop. Everyone was telling me to eat some breakfast, telling me I needed to eat. I knew they were right, but I just didn't feel like it. I couldn't stomach the thought of eating. They convinced me to sit down and gave me a plate of food. For them, I ate two bites of eggs.

On the second bite, my brain flashed on this image of Dan: I was pregnant, and like all pregnant people, I was sensitive to smells. One morning, I came downstairs and Dan had just finished cooking eggs. In that moment, eggs became the worst smell on the entire planet and I started yelling at him, "Get that smell out of here or I am going to puke! I mean it, Dan, I can't stand that smell! I swear if you don't get those out of here, I will throw up all over." Dan looked at me bewildered; the day before I had loved eggs. Heck, twenty minutes before, when he said he was going to go make them, I was cool with it. However, knowing better than to fight with a pregnant woman, he grabbed the plate of eggs and went outside. He then proceeded to stand in the window and stare at me, as he shoveled forkful after forkful of eggs into his mouth. He looked ridiculous, standing outside eating eggs while staring at me through the window. I laughed and laughed at him. That day was eight years ago. This day he was dead.

I started choking on my eggs and spit them up while someone was patting my back. I knew I wasn't up to eating.

Somewhere in all this more phone calls were made. I personally called another best friend, Jill. She lived eight hours and another time zone away in Boise, Idaho. When Dan and I were in college, Jill and our other friend Katie were our best friends; the four of us did everything together. I remember it was pretty early when I called Jill because I wanted to catch her before she went to work. Her husband answered the phone.

"Hi Jeremiah, is Jill still home? I need to talk to you guys." I don't know if he could tell from my voice that something was wrong. I tried to sound steady. He put it on speaker phone and I told them what happened. I don't remember what I said. Seizure...911...couldn't save him...died...Dan died. All I remember is Jill saying my name over and over slowly, "Jenny...Jenny...Jenny," and then what were quickly becoming my favorite words: "We're coming."

I made one more phone call to our other best friend from college, Katie. She lived in San Diego. Dan was supposed to fly down that day for work. They were going to meet up for dinner, so she kept calling Dan's phone to finalize plans. She was nine months pregnant and I was concerned this news would send her into labor, but I couldn't ignore the phone anymore.

"Hi Katie...how are you feeling? How's the baby? I need you to go sit down, okay? Dan isn't coming today... Seizure...911...died...Dan died." She said she had to go, and she hung up the phone. I heard later, that she went to her husband's work.

More people came to my house: friends, family, my pastor. As introverted as Dan was, he would have been freaking out at the amount of people that were crammed into our tiny house that day. India played outside with some friends. I kept asking about her, but she seemed okay. My dad called Dan's boss, my sister Desi called India's school. I have no idea how either of those conversations went. I sat in the library with my dad, the pastor, and others. I guess we were planning a funeral. I got a phone call from the funeral home. They wanted me to come in that afternoon and make arrangements.

"Today? I have to do that today?" Don't they know my husband just died? Yes, they needed me to come in today. 3:00 PM.

"Bring the clothes you want him to wear," they said. Wear? Like to the funeral? Bring the clothes I wanted Dan to wear at his funeral? Did they really just tell me this? Something black, I guess? Dan's favorite color is black, he has a favorite black shirt, it's probably dirty, let me see if I can find it. I went into our bedroom and started digging through the dirty clothes looking for his shirt, so we could wash it. It didn't make a lot of sense to me to wash a shirt to bury Dan in, I mean certainly it was going to get dirty doing that. Nevertheless, I found the shirt and a pair of pants and handed them to somebody to wash. Black was Dan's go to color. He loved wearing black. Black shirt, black slacks, black shoes, black tie. Dan would be going to his own funeral all in black just like he liked.

I sat on my bed. A bunch of people were in my room. I don't know who or where they all came from, but we were all just hanging out on my bed. Everyone wanted me to rest before going to the funeral home. Are they kidding me? How the hell am I supposed to rest? Oh, no problem. I'll just take a little nap and then I will feel right as rain.

It was time to tell the world. I checked with my dad and Dan's mom, Pat, to make sure all the family had been told. Then I texted Dan's boss to make sure he had told everyone at Dan's work. Then I got on Facebook. I don't have to look up what I wrote; I remember exactly what I said. It was carved into my heart with a knife as I was typing the words:

> *This is Jenny. It is with an excruciating sad heart that I*
> *have to tell you Dan passed away extremely suddenly and*

unexpectedly last night. We have a tentative funeral planned for Saturday. More details to follow.

I handed my phone to Stacie and asked her to copy that on Dan's page and post it please. That was it. The whole world was about to see the most devastating news on Facebook. It is a great way to reach a mass amount of people. I neglected to tell them what happened, that he had a seizure, or maybe I did it on purpose, maybe I didn't have the strength to type it out. I think it was all I could muster just to say that he had died.

An entire entourage left my house to go to the funeral home. I think we needed three cars. Me, India (because she wouldn't leave my side), Melinda, my friend Jacque, and her two kids to help distract India. My best friend Mari, who said she was going to take notes because I wouldn't remember. My dad, because he has actual funeral planning experience. My pastor. Dan's parents and Dan's brother Jerry. India's entourage went to the park next door to play (Melinda had to pull her away from me) and my entourage followed the 34-year-old widow into the funeral parlor to make arrangements for her husband's funeral.

Are we doing cremation or burying? That's a good question. Dan always wanted us to be cremated and I always wanted us to be buried. We would go around and around about it, but, seeing as we thought we still had 60 years to discuss it, we never came to a conclusion. Now, for some reason, it was up to me. Nobody else had any input on this decision. It was my dead husband, so I had to decide. We ended up deciding to cremate him, but not until after the funeral so we could have a viewing and Dan could be at his own funeral. I didn't have anywhere to bury him, anyway. We never got around to picking out a cemetery.

At some point, I was asked a question I couldn't answer. I started crying hysterically and turned my head around to look at Mari. "I don't wanna play this game anymore," I cried. As in, I don't want to do this. I don't want to be here. Please, oh please take me home. Let me wake up. Something, anything to make this stop. I will never forget what she did. She looked me straight in the eye and in her "mom" voice, grounding and firm, but not harsh, she said, "Hey, it's not the funnest date we've ever been on, but I'm here with you." Since Mari lived in Seattle, I didn't get to see her tons so when she would come down, we would try to squeeze in time to hang out. We called these times our dates. The last one we had was getting drive-through coffee and drinking it while going on a 45-minute drive to pick up her daughter from grandma's house. Exciting, right? We would have given anything to be doing that again instead of sitting at the funeral home talking about dead Dan.

Her assurance that she was with me helped me push through the rest of the arrangements. Mari gave the funeral director the bag of clothes we brought. I made more decisions I didn't want to make, and we talked about money. Funerals, it turns out, are expensive. We would be back Friday afternoon, for a private family viewing.

For some reason I had promised India that after I was done with my "meeting", we would go and get milkshakes and french fries. I guess I was trying to make the day fun or something, and what's more fun than milkshakes and fries? The entire entourage walked about a block away to Mike's Drive In, the hamburger restaurant that we frequented a lot in high school. They have great milkshakes. I ordered everyone milkshakes and fries. I just sat and stared at mine. I don't even know if I had one bite. I got a phone call from a lady in our church. I didn't want to talk, so I handed the phone to my pastor. I could hear him in the background talking, "Dan Stults died last night..."

We went home. I sat in the back seat of our minivan with India. The minivan that was near death, that had broken down the week before. I had just convinced Dan that we could afford a car payment and we should go shopping for a new minivan. Nobody would let me drive. I didn't want to anyway. India fell asleep on my shoulder in the car. That was good; she had only slept about one hour since Dan died. I wanted to sleep, too. When we got home, we could both go lie in bed. I carried her inside and there was a whole new host of people waiting to see me, waiting to talk to me, waiting to hug me. So, I sat on the couch and laid India on my lap. I was so tired. Was it midnight? No. It was only 5:00 PM. I don't know if I talked to any of those people. I just sat there. India woke up for a little while and then went back to sleep. I was able to lay her in my bed and come back out to the living room. I laid down on the couch; I couldn't keep my eyes open. The only people I remember there were my friends Mari and Shirley. I told them I wanted to go to sleep, they helped me walk (yes, I needed help walking) to my room and put me into bed.

The rest of the week is a complete blur. More snippets. Mari and I sat on the couch at 5:00 in the morning as I dictated what I wanted the obituary to say. I was surrounded by people. Every time I turned my head, someone was there. They were all looking at me like I was supposed to know what to do. I had no clue what to do. I sat on the couch looking through pictures, trying to find one for the front of the funeral program. I chose one of my favorite pictures. It was of the three of us a couple Christmases before. India and I were piled on top of Dan and we were all laughing. It's a great picture. I have never looked at it the same, though.

My cat kept getting in everybody's way. He kept sitting right in the walkway in the living room. Everyone would trip over him and say, "Ugh, Cat! Why are you sitting there? Move," as they tried to push him aside with their foot. The cat wouldn't budge. It took me until after the funeral to figure it out. The cat kept sitting in the spot where Dan died. The cat would not leave that spot. Dan got me that cat eight years earlier. I kept telling him I wanted a fluffy cat, so he got me an orange fluffy cat. His heart always belonged to Dan though. He was going to sit there until Dan came back.

On Tuesday, two days after Dan had died, still in a state of absolute shock, we went to the florist for funeral flowers. Before we left, I asked India (who was literally running away whenever I mentioned anything about Daddy's funeral) if she wanted a certain type of flower. She got a giant grin on her face, threw her hands in the air and said, "Daffodils!"

Daffodils?

"DAFFODILS!" Okay. Daffodils it is.

My dad, who is a gardening expert, leaned over to me, "Jen, it's January. I don't think you can get daffodils yet."

I answered harshly, "India wants daffodils. We are getting daffodils." Away to the florist we drove, with India, my dad, and some friends. I told the florist we needed daffodils. "DAFFODILS!" India cried, as she threw her hands up in the air and ran off to look around the store. The florist very gently explained to me that daffodils don't make very good corsages or boutonnieres. I replied, "That's my daughter over there, and she wants daffodils at her Daddy's funeral, and we are having daffodils. Okay?" I also got a big bouquet of daffodils for the casket.

"OK, Baby Girl, we got daffodils for Daddy's funeral."

"DAFFODILS!" she squealed, as she threw her hands up in the air. Daffodils for the funeral. Happy, like India. Full of life, like India. Fitting. Dan would never have picked yellow or daffodils, unless India wanted him to. He would do anything to make her happy.

My dad wanted me to pick colors for tablecloths. I didn't care. My sister wanted me to decide what to put in the program. I didn't care. There were so many people in my house. I kept thinking how it would have driven Dan nuts to have all these people in his house, but he wasn't here to be bothered by it. People kept asking me what I was going to do now. Hell if I know.

We went between my house and Dan's parents' house a lot. Food magically appeared in front of me; dishes got magically cleaned. Did I mention the people everywhere? They were all trying very hard not to bother me, but at the same time I was being asked a million and a half questions because I was the only one who could answer them. Anything from "where do the knives go?" to "what are you going to do for income?" I knew where the knives went.

Friday came. We had a private viewing for just the family. I have five siblings and Dan has five siblings, with spouses, the family is twenty people easy. I told India what we were doing and that she could choose if she wanted to go in the room and see Daddy, or if she wanted to go to the park with Auntie Melinda. I told her this early in the day, so she could have time to think it over.

When we got to the funeral home about half of the family thought I should make India go in, and about half thought I shouldn't. I was very determined that whatever happened, it was India's choice. I don't know how or when I decided that, but I did. Her dad was dead, she got to do whatever she wanted or didn't want to do. I know that's what Dan would have said about it.

In the midst of my giant family, I stopped and kneeled down to India's height. Looking her in the eye, I said, "Okay. Everybody is going to go into the other room and see Daddy. Daddy is dead, so it will look like he's sleeping in a coffin. Do you want to see Daddy, or do you want to go to the park with Auntie?" She opted to go to the park with Auntie, which was good because I totally lost it.

They opened the door to the room, and the family started to slowly walk in. I felt like I was being pushed along. I wasn't moving my feet, but I was still going forward. My dad was right behind me. I turned around and buried my head in his chest. I started screaming and crying, "I don't want to do this, I don't want to be here!" Yet here I was. I gave India a choice, but I didn't give myself a choice. I didn't have a choice. My dad told me something I don't remember and someone, I think my sister-in-law Dina, took my wrist. I was being pushed along with the crowd into the room again.

It was there, a brown wooden coffin. I don't think it's exactly what Dan would have picked out, but then it didn't matter. He was dead. Technically I picked it out. My brother in law narrowed it down to three choices he thought suited Dan: simple, natural, not overstated. I said something like, "Uh, that one," as I pointed.

Dan would have said, "Don't bother with a coffin at all. You know I want a Viking funeral, Jennifer. Stick my body on a raft and push me out to sea, then light it up with flaming arrows." I know he wanted a Viking funeral, but we didn't really have a lot of time to prepare. You need to get permission for things like that nowadays. We probably would have had to wait 60 days for a permit or something, and a Viking funeral was a lot of work. I guess he was in the one I picked, I couldn't really say.

I was led up to the coffin by Dina. I didn't want to go but I knew I had to. I couldn't look at him straight. I kind of looked halfway at the floor, and halfway at him. I started crying, "Why did you do that, Dan? Why? Why did you go and do that?!" I was so mad at him, like it was his fault. Like he died on purpose. I know he didn't, but I asked him anyway. I couldn't look directly at him and my eyes were blurry again. I asked Dina if everything looked right.

"Are his glasses on right? Are his earrings in? Does his hair look right?" She said yes, everything looked good. I noticed out of the corner of my eye that his nose looked purple. That wasn't right, his nose was always bright red from his allergies, his nose should be red. He had punctures on his wrists from where they embalmed him, it looked a little vampirish. I wish Dan were a vampire; then he wouldn't really be dead. He would be undead, not the same as alive but I would have taken it. Besides, I always said that in his prom picture he looked like Brad Pitt in *Interview with the Vampire*.

There were chairs and couches in the visitation room, and someone lead me to one. We sat there for I don't know how long. I don't remember anyone talking. We just sat, crying. Finally, Dan's mom said that she was ready to go. Dan's brother Jerry came over to me and handed me something.

"I was wondering if you would be OK if we put this on his coffin?" It was a bumper sticker, the same bumper sticker he had given Dan years ago. Dan loved that bumper sticker. It said, "I'm the Christian the devil warned you about." Yes Jerry, perfect. So Dan. I put the sticker on the back of his coffin, crooked of course. I can't make a straight line with a ruler. We went home. My sisters were still staying at my house. No one wanted to leave us alone. I didn't want to be left alone. I guess we went to bed. That's the logical conclusion. We had a funeral to go to the next day.

We woke up early again. Too early. We were not sleeping much or at all. Melinda and I packed up the car with things for the funeral: Dan's jacket, a quilt his mom made him out of his old t-shirts, pictures, our family scrapbooks that I loved to make. We got dressed in our funeral clothes and we got in the car to go to the church. My sister drove (they still were not letting me drive). India and I hung out in the reception hall. I didn't want her seeing them bringing Dan's coffin in. Somebody took our picture. It is really a good picture of the two of us. We were smiling. One of those automatic responses; whoever took the picture probably said smile, and so we did. What else are you supposed to do?

Dan loved tattoos and had many. It was one of his goals to cover his body in tattoos, but he never got that far. Melinda came up with a great idea. "We should have a temporary tattoo table at the funeral. Everyone who comes can put on a tattoo for Dan." So that's what we did. Everyone who came to the funeral got a tattoo for Dan.

India had already plastered herself with fake tattoos before anybody got there. It was a great idea.

It was time to close the casket; did we want one last look? I told them to wait and I went to find India. She was in the reception hall eating cookies with Melinda. I kneeled in front of her and told her they were going to close Daddy's coffin, and if she wanted to go see Daddy and say goodbye this was her chance, because we would never see Daddy again until she was an old, old grandma and went to heaven. People were trying to pressure her to go, but I was determined that it be her decision and hers alone. She may only be seven, but she gets to decide if she wants to look at her dead father or not. She very decisively shook her head yes. I picked her up and she laid her head on my shoulder. I walked down the hall.

In those few minutes, the church had filled up completely. There was standing room only and it was spilling out into the hallway. It was estimated that 400 people were at Dan's funeral. We had to sort of push our way through the crowd, like a police car on a jammed freeway. It wasn't that they weren't trying to move for us, it was that they had nowhere to go. As I walked, it felt like the whole church had turned to look at us. They probably did. India and I were all the rage that day. We made it up to the casket and I said something like, "See? Daddy just looks like he's sleeping." We stood there for a minute. My sister said India asked a question about his legs or shoes, because the lid was down on the bottom half of the casket. I told India to wave bye-bye to Daddy. She cupped her hand like a toddler would do and moved the tips of her fingers up and down. A shy little wave. Not a big happy "Swing me up in your arms, Daddy!" wave like she always did. Daddy couldn't swing her up in his arms anymore, and she knew it. She put her head back on my shoulder and I walked away. That is the last time we ever saw Dan.

I have this fantasy of being remembered, that my children's children will speak of me, and tell their children about what I have done. But this is a myth. I do not remember my great-grandfather's name, nor do I know what he did or what he was like, and I certainly know nothing of his hopes and dreams and if any of these were achieved. Chances are it will be the same for me.

Dan wrote that. I think he's wrong though. I think he will be remembered. I will remember him.

I was told I should have a designated person to be with India, in case she wants to leave at any time. That was a hard one. Anyone she was that comfortable with, like Grandma or Auntie, needed to be at the funeral. Luckily, one of my besties, Shirley, volunteered for the job. I think she knew that keeping India safe for me was more important than her attending the funeral. India had known Shirley her whole life. As the procession started, I gave India a choice again: did she want to stay with Mommy or did she want to go play with Shirley? This time she wanted to stay with Mommy.

A few days before the funeral I wrote on Facebook, "I know people have mixed feelings about bringing children to funerals. Please know that if your child is up to it, they are more than welcome to attend. I think it will make India not feel so alone to see other kids missing her Daddy. Dan loved children and I know he would want them there also." Somewhere around 30 children came to Dan's funeral: friends, classmates, relatives. All there to be with India. All there because they too loved Dan.

"I want to go play now." India said as soon as we sat down. I said okay, and I walked her down the aisle until we met Shirley who took her to play. I'm told the majority of the children there followed India out of the sanctuary, and they had a raucous party running around in the basement.

A lot of people talked: my pastor, my dad, my sister-in-law. We had an open mic for people to tell stories, and lots did. I don't remember what most of them said. I remember my dad ending his eulogy with, "If my other sons-in-law take care of their families even a quarter as well as Dan took care of his, they will be doing an amazing job."

I remember staring at Dan's coffin. We had laid a blanket over the top of it. India had gotten it for him a couple Christmases ago. It was gray and in navy said "I Love Dad" over and over and over again. On top of the blanket was the bouquet of daffodils India had picked out and one purple rose from me. I stared at the blanket, not the coffin itself. I stared at the daffodils, not the purple rose; which was the symbol of our love. I couldn't look at those things.

I had written a small eulogy. I didn't need to. I'm not a speaker. That was also Dan's forte, but I wanted them to know how much Dan loved us, how much he loved them. I had to let everyone know one more time. I didn't want them to forget. I walked up to the podium, my dad holding on to me because he was afraid I couldn't walk by myself. I'm not sure who was holding who up. He needed me as much as I needed him.

We had a funeral for Dan Stults, my 36-year-old husband who wanted to change the world. He wasn't sick, or hurt, or in an accident, he just had this tiny little seizure and died. I think half the church was expecting him to pop out of his coffin and yell "Surprise!" Then, he would jump up to the podium and give an amazing sermon about love and God and being there for each other in good times and bad. I know I was waiting for that to happen. But it didn't.

It seemed like all those 400 people wanted to talk to me at the reception. I have no idea what they said or even who a lot of them were. I don't remember any conversations, just looking at person after person talking to me. I just stared at everyone blankly. Did they think I was listening to what they were saying? I remember I was so thirsty I couldn't stand it. I was told that's from all the crying. My bestie Shirley walked by with a glass of water in her hands. I reached out and took it from her, downing the entire thing at once. The person I was talking to looked at me incredulously, like they couldn't believe I just stole that lady's water. Like it was the worst thing that had happened all day. I saw the look on her face and said, "Oh, it's ok. Shirley knows me well enough to share germs." I did not say, "We're at my husband's funeral, I've been crying for days, and I will drink whoever's water I want to."

We didn't go home after the funeral. We went to Dan's parents' house. Just the family and close friends, so only about 40 people. I don't know why we did that. It was better than going home, I guess. All I remember is sitting on the floor with my eyes closed while someone rubbed my back. Once again, people were everywhere. You could barely walk through the house, but it didn't matter. I was too tired to walk anyway. Dan's brother lived just down the road and he said if we went down to his house, he would light off fireworks he had left over from 4th of July. The BIG ONES. For some reason that sounded like the best idea ever. So, India, my sister, and I went down there. I don't remember if everyone else was too tired, or if we didn't even ask them. But we ended the day of the funeral watching fireworks explode in the sky. India and her cousins thought it was awesome and so did I.

On the one-year anniversary of Dan's death, I finally got up the courage to watch the video of the funeral. We videotaped it for Dan's grandparents who lived in Minnesota and couldn't travel, and for India in case she ever wanted to know. I'm not sure how to say this without sounding crazy, but watching that video was like having an out of body experience. I had no feeling attached to it. It just was. Like it wasn't me this was happening to; like it wasn't Dan in the coffin. It was more like I was watching a TV show. a bad one at that, because it wasn't grabbing me. I didn't cry, I didn't feel, I just watched.

CHAPTER 6:

The World Seemed to Burn

∞ ∞ ∞

Dan was cremated. That's what I, as his widow, decided. I had nowhere to bury him anyway. It took a week or two to "get him back". I remember calling the funeral home to check.

"So...when will my husband be back?" There's a loaded question. When my dad and I finally went to the funeral home to pick up his ashes, a huge rush of relief came over me as I held the box in my arms. Part of him, at least, was with me again. Dan's ashes were heavier than I expected. His body all fit into a plastic bag; it was tied with a round metal I.D. tag that had a number on it instead of his name. The plastic bag was inside a plain cardboard box, about the size of a shoe box, that stood upright. The box was wrapped in a light grayish blue paper with a gold seal on it and a white label that said Dan Stults. Proof that he's in there I guess. As we left, I told the funeral director, "No offense, but I really hope I never see you again." He probably gets that a lot. I put Dan in the back seat and my dad buckled him in for safety. We drove around with him the rest of the day, doing other fun errands like going to the Social Security Office.

Over the course of the next year, we did a lot of things with those ashes. I offered tiny jars of ashes to family members if they wanted some. I had a handful of places in my mind where I wanted to spread ashes. One day when I was ready (I have no idea how I decided I was ready, I just wanted to do it), Mari came over to help me separate the ashes into all these jars. I had read or heard somewhere that there could be pieces of bone or tooth that had not turned all the way to ash.

I told Mari, "There might be bits."

"Bits?"

"Yeah. You know. Like chunky bits."

"Okay..." she said, but clearly did not get my meaning. When we came across one of these "bits" she was surprised, which made me laugh at her.

"I told you there could be bits." She looked at me incredulously.

"Yeah, I didn't know that's what you were talking about."

We spent the afternoon scooping my husband's ashes out with a measuring cup and pouring them into small jars, while making jokes and comments about what he would be saying in this situation. It made it not so bad to laugh about Dan's ashes. What else is there? You laugh, cry, or both.

Today, what's left of my 36-year-old husband's ashes are in a beautiful handmade urn, on a shelf in the china cabinet he bought me one Christmas. I was so excited when I got that china cabinet, but of the million objects I thought I would put in there Dan's ashes never made the list. I always have the urge to point them out to people when they come over.

"Say hi to Dan; he's right there."

"Dan's just sitting around in the library; that's all he ever does anymore."

"There's Dan, you can yell at him if you want to. I do it all the time."

It lets people know I'm OK talking about him. Yes, that pretty jar is a dead person's remains. That way they don't have to wonder about it. Most importantly, it lets them know that I still miss him.

Next to it, in a smaller handmade urn, are more of his ashes. This urn was made specifically with India in mind. It is filled with her Daddy's ashes so that when she's older, she can do whatever she wants with them. She can take them with her to college, put them on the mantle of her first house, bury them in a cemetery and put up a head stone, peacefully spread them in her favorite place, or throw it against the cement in a rage so the urn breaks into a million pieces and his ashes fly everywhere. It wouldn't surprise me in the slightest if she chose the last option; I have contemplated it myself from time to time. When we finally got the urns, a year or so after he died, I showed them to India. I was excited to get them, but like all things to do with Dead Daddy she was in total avoidance mode. She literally ran out of the room and has never asked about them again.

At my in-law's house is another handmade urn with some of his ashes in it. They can do whatever they want with it as well; it appears they like it on their living room shelf. They made a memorial garden for Dan in their backyard, and we dedicated it by spreading ashes around at a family BBQ. I poured some from the jar into the hands of whoever wanted some and they sprinkled them around. Then we placed another very small jar in a niche in the garden wall. It was very solemn until I made a remark to my sister-in-law about her getting Dan on her pants. That made it better. Solemn doesn't really fit our family, and it doesn't fit Dan. Smart ass does.

On the eighteen-year anniversary of our first date I took three of my best friends: Stacie, Jacque, and Shirley, on a pilgrimage to spread Dan's ashes in two places. First, the spot where we had our first date, and then the church camp where we met. It was May 14,

2015, five months and two days since he died. Like all good pilgrimages we started out driving through our local Dutch Brothers coffee shop. The barista was trying to make small talk and asked what we were doing today. I hesitated, and she said, "Come on, it can't be that bad! I bet mine is worse!" Well, she asked.

"You really want to know?"

"Yeah!"

"Okay! We are driving to the beach to spread my dead husband's ashes." She agreed that I won the bad day contest and gave us our coffee for free.

First, we went just down the road from my house to the park where we had our first date. I walked around with my besties and tried to remember all the specific spots we stopped on a bench or bridge to talk. It was a bit hard because everything was so overgrown. Even though it was right down the road, this park had lost its funding and was in quite a state of disrepair. Because of this, we only took India to it once. It made Dan so sad that it wasn't cared for anymore. At the end of the trail was the small rock that I had stood on when we had our first kiss. It took a bit to find it because it was all overgrown with bushes. However, find it I did. I poured some ashes into my hand and placed my hand on the rock, remembering that kiss, the official start of our lives together.

We drove two hours to the beach, to the church camp where we first met. It had been twenty years since I had been there. When we got there, we went into the office. I told the clerk that this was where my husband and I met, that he had recently died, and I wanted to look around to remember him. I did not mention anything about spreading ashes. The lady at the desk gave me a very strange look, which to me did not seem very compassionate. she said, "Well, since there is no camp in session right now, I guess it will be okay." I guess I was expecting her to start crying, tell me to do whatever I wanted, and ask me to tell her all about Dan, but she didn't. She just gave us strange looks as we walked into the camp.

We walked down to the very picnic table I was sitting at when I first saw Dan. It was in the exact same spot, outside the cafeteria, next to the lake. We sprinkled ashes there, covertly so the maintenance people wouldn't notice. I just let them slip through my fingers. We walked to a deck overhanging the lake and spread some ashes there. They just sat on the top of the lake, sparkling in the sun. It looked more like glitter than ashes, which was funny because Dan hated glitter. Now, he was some. We walked to the campfire. It was not the same campfire. A building had been built over the campfire area, but the sentiment was the same. I went to the back row where Dan and I shared his blanket during campfires. I spread ashes in that back row. We walked up the hill separating the camp from the ocean and stood on the dunes. Dan and I sat here and talked and talked for hours. I poured more ashes into my hand and gently let them go into the wind. Again, the combination of sun and water made them look like glitter as they blew away.

Going to those places was not what I expected it to be. They were the same but not the same. Different. Older. Overgrown. Like us. I thought I would be crying all day, unable to drive or think. I didn't cry at all, only shed a few tears. I had this weird sense of peace, holding Dan's ashes in my hands, letting them fall between my fingers. I still tell myself a million times a day that this isn't real. This isn't my life. Dan isn't dead.

I didn't use up the entire jar of ashes I had for this pilgrimage, so when we got back to my car, I stuck the jar in that little place between the seats and under the dash. You know, where you stick things like hair ties and pens and Chapstick. It was the perfect spot for a dead husband to go. When we got back home, I started to clean out my car. I grabbed the jar to take him inside and then I thought, "No, I'll leave you in the car for a while. Never know where you might want to go." They are still there, three years later. They ride around with me all the time. He still doesn't like my driving, but he doesn't complain about it anymore.

I suppose it's weird to keep your dead husband's ashes in the car, but you know what's weirder? For the husband to up and die in the first place, blowing to pieces the life that you had together. THAT's weird. So, I keep some ashes in my car. I talk to them and maybe while I'm driving around, I'll think of a special place that I hadn't thought of before. It's also convenient to have him in the car with me when I feel the need to flip him off.

At his family's annual beach trip that summer we spread more ashes. Dan always wanted what he called a "Viking funeral". He wanted his body to be placed on a boat and pushed out to sea, then he wanted arrows of fire to be shot at him, catching his boat and body on fire as it sailed out to the horizon. We didn't do that for his funeral. Expenses, timing, and the lack of government approval all made it impossible. His mom and I felt a little bad about it, but only a little. Because really, Dan? Maybe if he had died in 60 more years, like he was supposed to, I would have been able to plan better.

At the beach, Pat made a tiny cardboard boat, like the size of a bath toy. In those days I was coloring rather feverishly in those adult coloring books. It was a form of therapy. It took concentration but not real thinking, so it was a good distraction. I took one of the pictures I colored and fashioned it into a small box to hold his ashes in the boat. The entire family walked down the beach to the little river that went out to the sea. India and I stepped into the river, and I lit the boat with a match and stuck it in the water. My sister-in-law started playing music from Braveheart on her phone. It was Dan's favorite movie. All the kids ran after the boat down to the ocean. It got hit by the first wave, and we watched as it toppled over into the sea. India was present but not present; like all situations having to do with Dan's death. She preferred to be off in her own world, in the background watching, paying attention, but not really wanting to participate.

We went to Boise to visit our friends from college. Jill still lived there, and Katie came up from San Diego. The four of us did everything together in college; we were a family. We had a small picnic with everyone that still lived in our college town. I hadn't seen some of them in over ten years. Afterward, anyone who wanted to drove up to an overlook in the foothills that has a view across the entire city. Dan and I loved going up there. It was a special place for us. We all walked to the edge to spread Dan's ashes over the city.

I opened the jar of Dan's ashes. They were stuck. They had apparently compacted during the drive from Oregon to Idaho. They wouldn't pour out. We were on top of a mountain, and I didn't have a knife or anything to loosen them. There were no sticks or branches I could use, either. So, I used my finger. I stuck it in the jar and started to dig at Dan's ashes with my fingernail. It was harder than I expected; they were compacted pretty well. I got ash under my fingernail, but I loosened enough to spread some into the wind. It felt like it took forever as everyone was staring at me, but in reality, it was probably only a minute. I tipped the jar and Dan's ashes came falling out into the wind. They blew into the city. Again, I felt a peace in doing it, sort of like Dan was a part of it, a part of us again, if just for a second. Dan and I never really felt like we belonged in that city, but we did. We left a mark there. Dan's ashes belong there, looking after all the lost kids.

India was there (but not there) in the background playing with the other kids, not paying attention to the grownups. Not wanting to be a part of saying goodbye to Daddy. Jill's husband was keeping an eye on her for me. He knew that was important: keeping India safe for me so I could do what needed to be done.

After that I sat on a bench between Jill and Katie. It was seven months after Dan died and the first time in nine years that the four of us had been together. Except Dan wasn't really there, just his ashes. The three of us sat and looked at the stunning view. We held hands and cried together. We were all mourning Dan together and I really needed that. The family we had made for ourselves was missing our beloved Dan. We would never be the same again, and the three of us understood that all too well. Jill asked me later what my favorite part of the weekend was. I told her that it was sitting up on Table Rock with her and Katie, all holding hands, all missing Dan together.

The next day we went to our old college to reminisce. We stood in front of my old dorm. When Katie met Dan, he was dancing around the pole in front of that room, waiting for me to come out. It was quite a first impression for her. So, we spread some ashes there. We spread some ashes on the spot where Dan and I buried our beloved cat when she died, because we were living in an apartment and had no ground of our own. We never told the school we did that. We spread some ashes outside the classroom buildings where we had spent so much time learning. We put some in a board game in the rec room because it was funny. Dan would have done it.

We took ashes to his grandparents' house in Minnesota. We spread them over his grandmother's grave. India was standing downwind, again in the background, present but not. The wind blew the ashes into her face. She sputtered, wiped her face with her hand and giggled. I laughed it off as well. "Look Daddy was giving you kisses," I said. I was trying to make it normal that she would have her dead father's ashes on her face. I think it worked.

When my youngest sister, Melinda, got married, we took a jar of ashes. Our sister Pauline even made him dress up, by making a tie out of paper and sticking it on the jar. He hated ties but he would have done it for Melinda without complaining. She wanted him at her wedding. Before the ceremony, Melinda, her fiancé Kyle, and I all snuck off with the photographer. I poured some ashes into each of their hands and they stood on a bridge across a stream and let his ashes go. They floated down the stream to where the wedding would be held. As with every time we have spread his ashes, a strange feeling of peace came over me and I felt closer to him. Almost like he was there. Then Kyle sang a little song that went, "I've got you in the palm of my hand, Dan." We all laughed. I am pretty sure we totally weirded out the photographer, but that's her problem, not ours.

Dan was supposed to officiate their wedding, like he did for Pauline. I was a bridesmaid and India was the flower girl. We were all supposed to be up there on her wedding day. Dan couldn't officiate because he was dead. Melinda knew it wasn't right that Dan wasn't up there with the rest of us. She wanted Dan in her wedding, and she was going to make it happen. She took the jar of ashes and held it in her hand next to her bouquet when she walked down the aisle. Our dad and Dan walked Melinda down the aisle on her wedding day. It was the next best thing to having him there. When she got to the front, Dan's ashes were passed to me and I held him there through the rest of the wedding. I spent the entire day holding his little jar of ashes. He was in all the family photos, although I don't think you can see him in there since he was in my hand. At the reception he sat on the table next to me, quiet, but there.

I spread some ashes in the backyard of our old house before we moved, just me, just one day as I was packing up. I wanted to leave some of him there, in the house where we had such precious wonderful memories, and one extremely bad one. Part of him belonged there in that house. I spread some ashes in the backyard of our new house when we moved. Just me, casually, as I was unpacking. I wanted him here with us in our new house. I wanted him here to make memories with, and this was as close as I was going to get.

There was too much of him to keep in one spot, in one jar. He would have hated it. His life meant too much to too many people for me to keep him all to myself. I had to spread him around; it was the only thing to do. I have a few more spots I want to spread his ashes. I just haven't gotten there yet. At most of the places I spread ashes, I had whoever I was with take pictures. I somehow had the presence of mind to know I would not remember, and I wanted to remember. Some of them turned out quite beautiful. I put them in a photo album with the funeral pictures. My mother in law asked me how I could stand to spread ashes and make a photo album like that. How could my heart take it? I told her that it actually made me feel better. I didn't really know why. Then a very wise friend said, "Well, that makes perfect sense! It's because you are doing something with him instead of everything you have to do without him." It does make sense. In the crazy widow world I live in, it makes sense. I don't know if other people will get it, but it doesn't matter if they do or not. I was doing something with my husband again. I wanted that more than anything.

I am still waiting for Dan to walk through the door. I can see him. I can picture his hand turning the knob. It's the first thing I see as the door slowly creaks open. He has black hairs on his knuckles and on his wrist going up his arm. I know the size of his hands and the only way I can describe them is to say they are slightly bigger than mine. Mine fit into his perfectly, that's how I know they're his. He has big knuckles from a lifetime of popping them. I hated it when he popped his knuckles, or his knees, or his back. I hate that sound. I miss that sound.

I hear two things. I can hear the sound of his keys as he puts them into his pocket. They sound just like anybody's, but these have the distinctive sound of Dan's keys. He doesn't have any key chains on his key ring, just a bunch of keys. I'm pretty sure half of them go to nothing. He probably still has the keys to the swimming pool where he worked in high school. I also hear him sniff. If I couldn't see or hear anything else, I would know him by his sniff. He had constant allergies and would sniff hundreds of times a day. India has inherited the same allergies and the same sniff. As he's sniffing, his hand goes up to his nose and he pushes the side of it with his knuckle. Trying to keep it in, I guess? I don't know, I never asked. Why would I? It was just a tiny thing he always did that no one ever noticed. I noticed.

I can see his face. He is looking down toward the ground. It makes his eyelids look closed, and I can see his long, long lashes flicking To me he is always clean shaven, although he had a beard for years and years. I would always complain that it was itchy when he kissed me. His hair is brown and tied back in a ponytail at the bottom of his neck. He has long hair, longer than mine. It was starting to recede in the front, slowly inching its way back. He also has a few grey hairs on the side above his ear.

Then I can see his whole body for the first time. He has on his favorite clothes. Tennis shoes, khaki slacks, and a black t-shirt with a saying on it. "Comfort the disturbed, disturb the comfortable" was his favorite, so I had him wear it to his funeral. This is what he wore almost every day. He hated jeans and didn't own any. He only wore button down shirts if he had an important meeting that day. I know the size of his body, I know the shape. The best way to describe it is slightly bigger than me so that I fit into him perfectly. His stomach has grown some since we first got married, but that's OK. Mine has, too.

This all takes place in a matter of seconds. Walking through a door only takes a second. Then, he looks up at me. He has this look on his face that's saying, "What? Why are you looking at me so funny? What!" Like it's no big deal. Like he hasn't been dead for two years. Like I just saw him this morning and now we are meeting up for lunch. Like he just kissed me goodbye and now he's going to kiss me hello. Just like it was yesterday. There's a sparkle in his eye like he really knows he's tricking me, but he isn't going to give up the game. I can still picture him perfectly, but he hasn't been here for two years now.

CHAPTER 7:

Push Away the Unimaginable

∞ ∞ ∞

My therapist told me once that my story would make a "really good, bad Sandra Bullock movie". I think she may be right. This is the chapter that earns that title. When Dan died, other things died too. I don't talk about it as much because, although it is a huge life shattering loss for me, it is nothing compared to having Dan die. So many of our hopes and dreams died with him that I can't even count them all. Some were minuscule, and some were so huge that, until Dan died, I thought they meant everything.

Dan and I wanted babies so badly. I wanted four and he only wanted three. We would tease back and forth about why one was better than the other. I would end it by saying, "You just wait and see, I'm going to win this one!" We also knew that we wanted to adopt someday. Even before we were married, we talked about how we felt that adopting was something we were meant to do. We weren't entirely sure what that looked like. Maybe we would have a couple kids and then adopt a couple. Maybe we would only adopt one, but we knew we would have children through adoption. It's one of two things in my life that I was sure God wanted me to do. The other was to marry Dan.

When we found out I was pregnant with our daughter, we were ecstatic. We could not wait for her to get here. My body, however, was less than happy about the new occupant. I did not take pregnancy well. I was sick and miserable all the time. All I did was go to work, come home, go to bed, and stay there. Dan took care of everything. He did all the cooking, cleaning, and laundry for nine months. All while catering to me, working, going to school, and doing his internship. When I would tell him how sorry I was for not helping more, he would stop me mid-sentence, look me in the eyes, and say, "Hey, you are growing our baby. That is way more important than anything else, and it is the only job you have to worry about. I will take care of everything else." My body's intense hatred for pregnancy culminated in premature labor. I thought it was a stomach ache, but Dan saw it for what it was: contractions. We rushed to the hospital, where we were taken by ambulance to another hospital with a NICU. The doctors were certain I was going to give birth in the next 24 hours. Luckily, doctors can be wrong. I stayed in the hospital for fifteen days, on lots of lots of medication, to stop my labor and keep India safely in the womb. It worked. I was released on strict bed rest, where I stayed for two months until she was born just days before her due date, in perfect health and way too smart. Just like her Daddy.

I have never seen Dan more terrified in my entire life than the night at the hospital when he knew there was a possibility that his wife and baby could die. He was always so calm and collected, but that night, even I, in labor and on more medication than I can remember, read the utter terror in his eyes. It's ironic, isn't it? Dan was afraid I was going to die. Really, really afraid. And then it turned out he died instead.

After that, we decided this pregnancy stuff was not all it was cracked up to be, and we would adopt the rest of our children. We were excited. Adoption had always been in our plan. When India was three years old, we were ready for another baby and started the adoption process.

When she was four, we were placed on the waiting list for a domestic infant adoption. Those happen in one of two ways: either a birth mother chooses you to adopt her child or you get a call from a hospital for a baby that has been given up. We waited, and we waited, and we waited. We did fundraiser after fundraiser; over two summers, I organized six giant rummage sales to pay for our adoption. Dan hated them because we had to store all the stuff for weeks ahead of time. We had boxes of junk all over our house. I assured him it would be worth it when we had our baby.

For reasons I do not know, we were passed over by birth mother after birth mother. So, we continued to wait. All three of us were feeling stressed and frustrated at the waiting. I kept telling myself that God was allowing us to wait so long, because our new baby was going to be truly amazing. Maybe we were even waiting for twins or triplets! Then we wouldn't have to go through the whole adoption process again; our family would be complete in one swoop.

We decorated the nursery. My sister painted Narnia themed murals on the walls, just as she did with India's baby room. Aslan was above the crib watching over the baby. We set up a changing table and a dresser. In the nursery was the rocking chair Dan got me on my first Mother's Day. We both spent hours rocking India in that chair, and we were ready to do the same for our next baby.

I had saved all of India's baby clothes, just in case the new baby was a girl, and if it was a boy maybe the one after that would be a girl. We had tubs and tubs of clothes. I also started buying gender neutral baby clothes that I just couldn't resist.

I was very big on trying to find ways for India to be involved. We spent years telling our daughter what an awesome big sister she was going to be. She could help feed the baby his bottles and sing him to sleep. I made a little picture book for her to help explain the adoption process. She completely rolled with the adoption. It was as natural to her as it was for us; of course we were adopting a baby, what other way was there to get one? I had a plan to have her decorate certain bottles, so they would be the special ones that would only be used when India fed the baby. I made the baby a blanket and pillow and then made India a pillow to match. When we painted the baby room, I gave her half a wall to paint whatever she wanted on it for the baby. She covered every inch of it in bright colors and hearts. I bought her two different shirts that said "I'm the Big Sister". She outgrew them both before she ever got to wear them. When India was a baby, she had pacifiers that said "I Love Mommy" and "I Love Daddy" on them. While waiting for our adoption, I had pacifiers made that said "I Love India". I never showed them to her; I wanted to surprise her when the baby came.

Every time I went to the store, I would take a leisurely walk through the baby section to be sure we had everything we absolutely needed, and make a list in my head of what I still wanted to get. I even made a baby registry at several stores. I bought a diaper bag with a teddy bear on it. I love teddy bears, plus it would work for a boy or a girl. I bought diapers, wipes, and formula. We were going to need so many of those things, and I wanted to be ready because we could get a call at any moment. It wouldn't do to have to stop by the store to pick up diapers on our way to the hospital to meet our child.

Dan didn't stop me. It distracted me from the stress of waiting. I had an infant car seat in the closet all ready to go, but he did refuse to let me strap it into the car. I tried to argue with him.

"What if we are out somewhere and we get a hospital call? We will need the car seat!"

"Then someone can bring it to us," he replied. We were completely ready for this baby. Why wouldn't we be? By this time, we had been waiting for four years.

My life happens to, on occasion, suck beyond the telling of it.

— Buffy the Vampire Slayer

I was sitting on our bed, roughly 12 hours after Dan died, when I got a phone call. We had just finished finding clothes for Dan to wear to the funeral when I collapsed on the bed, in shock, trying to make sense of what I had just done. I actually decided what my husband was going to wear as he lay in his casket, at his funeral, which was taking place only a few days from now. Now. When he was 36 and I was 34. That can't be right. I'm not supposed to be doing this now. I have at least 70 years before I need to do this. It felt like there were a million people around me, though in reality it was probably only four or five, crammed into our tiny bedroom. One of my best friends, Stacie, was sitting beside me. I don't know why except that's what she always does. She's great at sitting beside you.

I was holding my phone in my hand and it rang. I looked at it and it was our adoption agency. My first thought was, "Wow, they found out about Dan really quickly. I wonder who told them?" My second thought was, "I really do not want to talk to those people right now." Stacie gave me a look that said "just blow them off", so I handed her the phone. She could talk to them for me, thank them for calling, or whatever it is you do when people call to tell you they are sorry that your husband just died. I could hear Stacie in the background, but I wasn't really paying attention to what she was saying. Something about how, yes, I was here but couldn't talk and that she was a family friend. The case worker, for whatever reason, wouldn't talk to her, and Stacie reluctantly handed the phone back to me.

Then I found out why she wouldn't talk to Stacie. She needed to give me the great news herself. I have no idea what exactly she said, but it involved the words "Hospital", "Baby",

"Congratulations", and "Come get your baby". I couldn't believe what I was hearing! How was this possible? I started yelling into the phone, "He died last night! He just died! HE DIED! HE DIED! HE DIED!" I was screaming hysterically. Stacie took the phone out of my hand. I think maybe I stood up when I started screaming at our case worker. I don't remember standing up, but I remember sitting back down on the bed again. I heard my dad come racing down the hall. He told the people in the living room, "It's the adoption agency. They have a baby." How? How was this happening?

Through blurry eyes, I was looking at the floor of our bedroom. Dan's side of the bedroom. The floor where his unconscious body lay after I pulled it off the bed. I kept seeing his body. I would blink, and it would just be carpet, blink again, and his body was back. I was crying, "Dan. Dan, our baby is here. Where are you, Dan? Our baby is here!" I'm not sure if it was a whisper or a scream, but it sounded like both in my head. I was crying so hard I started to choke. I guess the other people in the room thought I was going to throw up, because someone grabbed the closest bucket and pulled it over to me. It was the laundry basket that I had just finished rifling through to find Dan's funeral clothes. If Dan would have still been lying on the ground, the basket would have cut through his legs.

The next thing I remember, I was lying in my bed with all the lights off and Mari was rubbing my back. Everyone kept telling me I needed to rest. Were they crazy? It was bad enough that Dan was dead, but this put in stark reality what I already knew: no Dan meant no more babies. This isn't my life; this isn't what happens to me. In my dreams, I have a houseful of giggling children, and their Daddy is wrestling with them on the floor. Now it's just India and me, and that's all. Dan was right. She had to be enough.

We didn't get to adopt that baby. It turns out they won't let you when your husband has just died and you're in no fit state to get out of bed, much less care for a newborn. A few weeks later I emailed our case worker, just one sentence: "What do we do now?" I knew it was going to be awful and I wanted to get it over with as soon as possible. We arranged a time for me to go in and officially close our account. I took Jacque with me for moral support. Still in complete shock from the sudden death of my husband, I was astounded at the lack of compassion from the people whose job it is to create families. My family was gone, so I guess I didn't count anymore. Or perhaps they just didn't know how to respond to me. It's probably rare for this to happen to people who have undergone physicals and mental evaluations and interviews. I suppose they don't just drop dead every day.

Technically speaking, I could still adopt from foster care or internationally, if I wanted to. I could do it all by myself, without my husband. It was up to me. They would put my account on hold for six months, by then I should be feeling up to it. After all, six months is so long. Surely, I would be fine by then. I knew that wasn't going to happen. I knew I would never feel up to adopting again. I couldn't do it without Dan, but what's more, I didn't want to. We were in this together. I didn't want to have kids without Dan. I didn't even want to raise India without Dan, but I was pretty attached to her by then. I had to tell them, physically say the words, "I don't want to adopt anymore." That way, I was changing my mind. They weren't forcing me to. All the blame was on me. They weren't liable. They didn't need to refund anything, or be compassionate, or help in any way, because I had changed my mind. The circumstances that caused me to change my mind didn't matter to them.

India never got to be the big sister she always wanted to be. She spent most of her life practicing with her baby dolls: feeding them, rocking, them, carrying them around everywhere. Baby doll car seats and strollers and highchairs were all over our house. One time I counted her baby dolls. She had 26. We spent most of her life telling her how great she was going to be at being the big sister. She talked about the baby we were going to adopt constantly. How she was going to feed it, burp it, sing to it while they rocked, and play with it. She was willing and excited to do everything except change the diapers. Mommy and Daddy had to do that. Dan and I encouraged her. We wanted her to be excited about being a big sister. She would hold friends' babies and we would ooh and aah at how cute they were. We would imagine all the mischief our children would get into together. We even talked about how when she was old enough, she could babysit her siblings while Daddy and I went out. She was all in, just like we were.

To my knowledge, India knows nothing about the phone call from our adoption agency. I'm not sure where she was when all that happened, but I think she was outside jumping on the trampoline with friends. I didn't tell her right away that we weren't going to adopt anymore. We had enough to deal with, and that could wait. Breaking the news to her was not quite as bad as telling her that Daddy had died, but it was a close second. I don't remember exactly what I said. I sat her on my lap, in the baby's room, in our rocking chair. We have had lots of important conversations in that chair, so she knew something was up. I said something about how since Daddy had died, we weren't going to adopt anymore, and I was going to start cleaning out the baby room. She said that she didn't want me to, but other than that, she pretended that the conversation never took place. That was typical of how India addressed her grief; she often ignored it completely.

Sometime later, I took her to her weekly therapy appointment. Her therapist spent about ten minutes talking to me, without India. She said I should talk to India about her not getting to be a big sister again.

"It needs to be addressed," she said. "Every time India plays with dolls in therapy, she has a Mommy, but no Daddy, a big sister and a baby sister."

The therapist deduced that she didn't quite understand that no baby was coming. This news broke my heart into even smaller pieces, and I started crying hard to the therapist. I felt like we had lied to India throughout her whole life. We didn't know we were doing it, of course, but we had gotten her hopes up so high. My hopes were up, too. I never thought our adoption wouldn't happen. I never thought death would get in the way.

Now I was going to have to tell her, again, that we weren't getting a baby. We were going to the beach the next weekend with Dan's family for the annual family beach trip, the first without Dan. We would also be spreading some ashes there, and it would be Father's Day, so we might as well have that conversation too. At least we would be at the beach. India and I could have this talk while we were playing in the sand and watching the ocean waves. We found a little pocket of water and stopped to play in it with her figurines of princesses, fairies, and mermaids. As we made a castle for them to live in, I talked to India. I told her that sometimes I was sad that we weren't going to have another baby.

She said, "But I thought I was your baby?"

"Yes," I said, "but I was so excited for you to be a big sister and now we aren't doing that." She shrugged. "You remember that we're not adopting a baby any more, right?"

"Yeah," she replied in a "duh, everyone knows that" way. That was the end of conversation. India then changed the subject dramatically, which was a clear sign that she was done talking about this.

The next day we were playing on the beach again. I started telling her how she was kind of like a big sister to her cousins and our friends' babies. I told her how that was pretty awesome, because, like being an auntie, it means you get to do all the fun stuff like play games and eat ice cream, but you don't have to do any of the icky stuff like listen to them cry or change diapers. I don't think she bought it. I didn't really buy it when I was telling her, but other people suggested it was a good idea, so I gave it a try.

I have five siblings. I never knew what it was to be alone as a kid. I always had someone to play with and fight with, and often it was the same person. I never had my own bedroom until Dan died. I went from sharing a room with my sister, to living in a dorm, to being married. India has always had her own room and doesn't know any differently. India doesn't know what it's like to have to share everything. I don't know what it's like to not share. Dan had five siblings as well, but they are stepbrothers and mostly lived with their mother, so he was often the only child. He always talked about how lonely his childhood was. This is why he made such a point of playing with India. I just shrugged at him. "She will be fine. As soon as we get the baby, she will have someone to play with."

I look into India's future, and it is so different than the one I imagined for her. Her sister won't be a bridesmaid in her wedding. She won't call them multiple times a day. When I am old and gray and need care, she will have to decide what to do with me all by herself. She won't have siblings to argue over what they believe to be best. She won't have anyone to give her breaks from sitting by my side in the hospital, if it comes to that. I wanted so badly for her to have siblings like I do.

My siblings are phenomenal. We have always been very close, but I would say we are even closer as adults. I always expected India to have a similar relationship with her siblings. That's what I wanted for India. I never expected for her to be an only child, but she is.

With Dan, I felt a great need to hang onto everything that reminded me of him. It was the opposite with the baby. I didn't want to be reminded of a baby we never had. I didn't want to acknowledge it. What I wanted was every trace of it gone, as soon as possible. I had that thought almost immediately after Dan's death, even before we got the phone call from the adoption agency.

The funeral home hadn't arrived at our house yet, and I was sitting in the rocking chair in the nursery, telling a social worker my name and address, and how many kids I had. I wonder if he thought I was pregnant, since we were clearly sitting in a nursery and there was no baby. As he was asking me questions, I was thinking about how everything in this room was pointless. I needed to get rid of it all. I wanted it all gone, right there, in that moment. Dan was dead, and I knew we would never get another baby. Why do I have all this stuff? It's pointless. It's all pointless.

Our friend Jill came over from Idaho the day after Dan died. They were staying for a week for the funeral. They had a nine-month-old baby girl. Sometime in that week the thought occurred to me that, since we were not going to have a baby, I should give them the clothes I had saved. At least someone will get some use out of them. Days after my husband died, I was rifling through our shed, looking for the tub of 12-month-old baby girl clothes. Then we sat in the living room while Jill went through the box and picked out what she wanted. I was very determined to do it and I didn't really understand why. Now I realize that it hurt too much to keep all that stuff around.

I also gave them some of the diapers and wipes I had been collecting. I gave other friends with babies more diapers, and more wipes. I donated all the formula to a women's shelter. I gave away what baby paraphernalia I could to friends that were pregnant and donated the rest to a thrift store. I wanted it gone. I wanted it all gone. I didn't want to look at it ever again.

As I was packing up our never-used baby room, there were some things I couldn't get rid of. I didn't want them, but I couldn't get rid of them either. I wanted these things to magically disappear: the diaper bag I bought specially, the custom pacifiers I ordered that said "I Love India", a blanket and a pillow I had made just for the baby, and a giant pile of adoption paperwork that we had poured our souls into. I put it all in a box and gave it to my sister-in-law.

"Here. Burn this," I said. She asked what was in it and I told her. Then she told me that she would not be burning it. We went back and forth a little bit, and I finally said, "Fine! I don't care what you do with it, but I never want to see it again!" She said she would keep it safe for me. I still think she should have burned it.

I wanted to paint over all the murals in the baby room. I wanted the room white, blank, empty, like the nursery had never existed. India would not hear of it. She loved those murals. They were very similar to the ones we painted in her baby room in the house we lived in until she was 4. I decided that she had been through enough lately, and that I could live with the murals.

Instead, I filled all the available space with pictures that Dan had kept in his office at work. I thought that at least that way, when I looked at the wall, I could focus on something other than the murals, and other than our nonexistent baby. I put in a table and some bookshelves. I moved the computer and printer in there. It was going to be an office now. I could get a work-from-home job, and that would be my office. I started referring to it as the office and correcting India when she said, "baby room."

"Oh, you mean the office," I would tell her. I was trying to fool myself, and it wasn't working. I couldn't be in there for more than a couple of minutes at a time. I couldn't concentrate on anything while I was in that room. I tried working in there, and it was impossible. It became a catch all storage room for all of our junk. I only went in there when I needed to get something, or when India wanted to rock in the chair. The rocking chair is the only thing I kept.

Twelve hours after Dan died, I lost a baby. Except it wasn't really my baby, but I had been hoping and praying for it, for way longer than it takes the average person to have a baby. Losing that baby was small, compared to losing Dan. That baby was never really mine, and Dan was. I had spent half my life with Dan. However, it was still a huge loss. We were right in the middle of the "growing families" stage of life. Five of our friends had babies within the first year of Dan's death.

One of my besties, Shirley, had a baby the August after Dan died. She was just barely pregnant when Dan died. Her older son is exactly nine months younger than India. I like to tease them that they came to the hospital to see India, and she was so magnificently perfect that they wanted one of their own. India and Zigo spent all of their infant and toddler years together. We always talked about how our second kids were going to be the same way, just months apart, built in playmates. It was going to be fantastic. That's how it should have happened.

Eight months after I got the phone call about our non-existent baby, Shirley called me. They were at the birthing center; the baby was born in the middle of the night. I was the first person she called, and she wanted me to come see the baby first. I wanted to throw up. I wanted to go hug her, and congratulate her, and hold her precious baby, but I didn't think I could make it out the front door. I suspect that India was having the same internal turmoil, because she kept telling me her tummy hurt. I had to go. I couldn't lose it now; I had to be there for my friend. So, I took some anxiety pills, and gave some to India, and we got in the car. I had to take anxiety pills to see my best friend's baby.

At the birthing center, India treated the situation how she treated everything at that time. She was there but not really there.

Staying off to the side, not wanting to be involved. She talked to her friend, their older son, and ignored the baby. I sat on the edge of Shirley's bed and her husband handed me the baby. I looked down at the baby.

"We were supposed to have babies together," I said.

"I know," Shirley replied.

"I'm trying really hard not to cry," I said.

"I know," Shirley replied. And we sat there, my friend and I, as I held her newborn baby and cried huge hard tears for the baby I was never going to have.

Life, death, and babies are always filled with what ifs. What if they had called us the day before? We would have been at the hospital with our new baby when Dan had his seizure and they would have been able to save him. He would have never died. We would have been celebrating our new baby's first birthday instead of mourning the one-year anniversary of his death. Three years after Dan's death I still think about that baby. I still wonder if it was a boy or a girl. Those thoughts are all wrapped up in the things we dreamed of that will never happen now: a big house full of kids, growing old together, sitting on the back porch holding hands while we watch our grandchildren play in the yard. All our dreams are nonexistent now, just like our baby, but they did exist. They used to exist. We had it all, for one second.

CHAPTER 8:

Stay Alive

∞ ∞ ∞

Everything here is hard, and bright, and violent.
— Buffy the Vampire Slayer

For months, and even more than a year after Dan's death, everyday life felt jumbled and chaotic, with no sense of direction. The idea that you will be done grieving after a year, that you will feel better once twelve months have passed, is a lie from the pit of hell. You won't and you don't have to. Waking up every day and realizing you made it through the night (which you weren't sure you wanted to do) and figuring out how to make it through another day is hard. It's all you can manage to just get up. Everything else is a cluttered, untidy mess. Unfortunately, it was my mess, and I had to try to make sense of it.

The first dream I ever had about Dan was months and months after he died. I was beyond exhausted. Every day was getting harder, not easier. Anyone that tells you that it gets easier is lying. It doesn't get easier. Especially not in the first 6 months, or the first year, or the first two years. Every day, more things were piling up. I was even exhausted in my dreams.

My exhausted body was dreaming that my exhausted body was in the kitchen, doing the dishes. I heard a noise coming from the living room, so I went to see what it was. As I stood in the living room, an invisible energy forced me to walk over and sit on the couch. I knew it was Dan, even though it was completely invisible. I just had a sense of Dan. He was telling me I was working too hard, that I needed to rest. When he was alive, he would do that sometimes. He would come into the kitchen, grab my wrist, pull me to the living room, and force me to sit on the couch. "You're working too hard, Jennifer. Rest. Relax. I've got this." As I sat on the couch in my dream the tears poured out of me. I was so tired. I was so sad. I couldn't even escape it in dreams. The invisible force that was Dan sat beside me. It didn't hold me. It didn't put its arms around me like Dan would have. Dan wasn't actually there, but his presence was there.

I woke up from that dream furious at Dan. I told all my friends about it and they said, "Sweetie, that is Dan telling you to rest. You need to rest." That just made me more furious. How dare Dan tell me to rest? I can't rest because he's not here to help me. It's his fault I'm so tired. I can't possibly rest. Maybe if he hadn't up and died on me, I would be able to rest.

I used to do this thing where I would walk around with my eyes closed. Not all day or anything, but while I was walking, I would close my eyes for a few steps. I'm not sure what I was doing. Trying to block out this crazy new world? Trying to block out the flashbacks of Dan dying? Trying to catch a breath? I know I was forcing myself to go on when my eyes couldn't take it anymore, so they just closed, while I kept moving. It had no rhyme or reason. I would do it at home, along the sidewalk, in the grocery store, at India's school. Maybe I was trying to keep myself from falling over or attempting to regain my balance physically and mentally. It seemed crucial to my survival. I wanted to close my eyes to the world, but I had to keep going. I had no choice. So, I would literally close my eyes and keep on walking It was the best I could do.

Most people think they can imagine what grief is like for the first couple of months. They imagine they'd be crying non-stop and unable to go out in public. Many people have told me, "If that happened to me, I would just lie in bed all day," or "I could never do that, I don't know how you do it." Maybe they are right. Each person handles life differently. Typically, though, my responses to those statements are, "No, you wouldn't; you have kids to take care of," and "Yes, you could. You don't have a choice."

People have also told me I have "handled this so well". Every time I hear that I laugh loudly in my head. Many times, I laugh out loud. Your tact tends to go out the window when you're grieving. Handled what well, exactly? My husband dying? My soulmate dying? My grief? My child's grief at the loss of her beloved father? My response has always been that I have no choice. I have no choice in any of it. I certainly did not have a choice in Dan dying. If I had, clearly I wouldn't have chosen it.

Grief is like living in complete emptiness. You don't feel anything, and yet you feel everything all at the same time. I burned my tongue on my coffee and didn't even know it. I stubbed my toe to the point of bleeding and I didn't notice. What I did notice was that it took all my concentration to breathe in and breathe out. Breathing has never been so hard. Breathing was exhausting. Breathing was so much work it took all my energy. I noticed that it felt like my heart was being ripped out of my chest constantly, over and over and over. My body was so beyond exhausted that my doctor wondered how I was functioning enough to get to her office. I don't know how I did it either, I just did. I just did what I needed to do to survive.

Then, there is this little seven-year-old with her Daddy's brown hair and her Daddy's stunning blue eyes. She nudges you in the shoulder and tells you she's hungry. You know, with every fiber of your being, that you cannot get out of bed to feed her. You are too tired to move. For the thousandth time, you wish her dad would help her, and for the thousandth time, you know he never will again. It's all on you; you must take care of her. Without knowing how, you push off the covers and put your feet on the floor. You have no choice. She needs you, and she is a part of him. It is harder than anyone can possibly fathom. I had to make myself do it, because I had no choice.

I got up and I took care of India in the best way I could, which was about 10% of what it was before, but I poured all my energy into making that 10% happen. We went from eating eggs and bacon every day to considering it a win if I could convince her to eat half a chocolate muffin.

We hung on. We went around in a fog and we hung on: to each other, to our blankies, to the side of the cliff we were dangling off. We hung on. We kept going. We did regular life things, simply because I didn't know what else to do. We went to barbecues and camping trips, playdates and coffee with friends. Every single second I thought about Dan: the night he died, all the things we would never do, his smile, his eyes. I was constantly missing him.

I had a sequence of three dreams. They were all mostly the same. I was at a giant party. All my family and Dan's family were there: siblings, parents, aunts, uncles, cousins. All our friends were there: high school friends, college friends, church friends, work friends. There were 300 people at least. It was a big room with lots of windows and the sun was shining in.

In the first dream, I was standing around talking to people when everybody started clapping and cheering. I looked, and Dan was coming out from around the corner. They were making a path for him, straight toward me. I saw him and fainted. When I opened my eyes, I was lying on the ground, and Dan was leaning over me

96

smiling with a twinkle in his eye and a mischievous grin on his face. It was like he was saying, "Haha, Jennifer! I tricked you good that time!" The dream ended before either of us could talk.

In the second dream, the setup was all the same. I was standing around talking, when everyone started clapping and cheering as Dan came into view. I saw him and ran straight toward him. I jumped into his arms, the way I used to when we were in high school, and we started kissing. We kissed and kissed, ignoring everyone around us. It was like a scene in a movie, where the focus is only on the main couple, and everything else blurs out. I could have kissed him forever, but that dream also ended.

In the third dream, the setup was the same once again. I was talking to people when Dan came around a corner. They all clapped and cheered as he walked toward me. I didn't faint. I didn't jump into his arms and kiss him. I started screaming at the top of my lungs. Everyone went silent while I screamed. Dan was cautiously walking toward me. He was trying to calm me down, but I couldn't hear what he was saying because my own screaming was too loud.

"No, it's not you! You're lying! This is someone else...it's not Dan! You're lying...you can't be Dan. Dan's not here. Dan died. He died! You're not Dan!" That dream ended as well.

Dan wrote me a letter once when I was out of town.

> *I miss you so much. I started missing you about the time you pulled out of the driveway. You know that loneliness feeling you get, the one that goes to the stomach first, and it feels like someone hit you there when you weren't looking or ready for it? Yeah, that feeling, that's the one I got. By Monday it had spread to my heart and that's where it sits now. I didn't think it would be this bad; perhaps it's because it's combined with the left behind feeling. I love you so much.*

Yes, Dan, I know that feeling. I know it better than you do now. That trip was a week. I've been missing you for years now. I have been left behind for years. It's one of the things I'm angriest about: being left behind. I want to be with Dan. I want to feel complete again.

I poured myself into reading things written for widows: books, blogs, articles, anything I could get my hands on that made me feel less alone. I craved things that I could relate to. I craved anything to help with the pain.

I found a widow writer named Catherine Tidd, and I fell in love with her writing. She was a smart ass and sentimental, like me. Her husband died suddenly, like mine did. She wrote this once and it sums up my feelings, exactly.

> *I just wanted to be with him. I was so homesick for him that it was a physical ache. And if he can't be with me...why can't I be with him? I wasn't feeling like I wanted to leave this world; I have a great life, wonderful kids, friends I adore, and I'm having a new sofa delivered next week. No, I don't want to die. I just want to be with my husband.*

Simple, right? Just being with your husband should not be so complicated. But the only way to achieve it is death, and that's just not an option. So, what does one do?

"You're doing it," says my therapist. Okay, then.

Another widow writer I relate to is Megan Devine. Her book is called *It's OK That You're Not OK.* I was reading her book when I came across a passage that really spoke to me.

> *For many people, continuing to wake up each morning is a disappointment. "Damn. I'm still alive." Thoughts like that make perfect sense. Feeling like you'd rather not wake up in the morning is normal in grief, and it doesn't mean*

you're suicidal. Not wanting to be alive is not the same thing as wanting to be dead. It's hard to tell non-grieving people that...

A few sentences later she writes,

Sometimes you do not care one bit whether you live or die. Not because you're actively suicidal, but because you simply do not care.

"This!" I said. "This!" I have felt like this so many times. More times than I want to admit, more times than I've told anybody about. I posted this in an online grief group and highlighted the passage I was referring to. Every comment said something to the effect of, "Me too! I feel this way, too!" Several people said it was so taboo they were afraid to tell their therapist. This is one of the deepest taboos about grief. It's the thing that nobody will talk about, not even with their therapists, but it's true. I simply did not care. If I lived, that was okay, I guess. If I died, at least I'd be with Dan.

It is a complex feeling, not caring. At least for me, because apart from that dead husband thing, I have a great life. I have a family that loves me unconditionally and I know would take care of me. Both my family and my husband's family would do anything for me. I have the most wonderful, kick-ass, amazing daughter that I love more than life itself. I have so many friends they are coming out my ears. I have a great home. Still, I did not care if I lived or died.

See, that dead husband thing is a big thing. In many ways, it voids out all the other great things. Dan was my soul and my life; he meant everything to me. Then, one night out of nowhere, he died. I just stood there and watched the love of my life die. That made me stop caring about anything anymore. I knew I should care, I knew all those other great things in my life to care about were still there, but it didn't matter. It made no difference to me whether I lived or died. Sometimes I think the only thing stopping me from actually wanting to be dead was India. I thought she might need her Mommy.

For months? A year? More than a year? I don't remember how long, but it was a long time. I would wake up every day and think, "Damn. I'm still alive." I was continually surprised. I couldn't fathom how Dan could be dead, and I could still be alive. I don't know how my heart is still beating when it is so completely shattered. One of my favorite lines is from the movie *Fried Green Tomatoes*:

> *A heart can be broken, but it still keeps a-beatin', just*
> *the same.*

My heart was shattered, but it still kept beating. It doesn't make any sense. Why don't I just drift off in my sleep? Why don't I just wake up in heaven with Dan holding me? Why am I still alive?

"Well, you're heartbroken," my therapist says. Uh, duh! Did it take you that long to catch on?

"Yes exactly," I say through tears. I am so heartbroken that it physically hurts, every day. The pain is horrendous. We were not a couple who had grown apart. We didn't fight. We weren't mad, or angry, or bitter at each other. We were madly in love with each other. Happily, ever after. And then we weren't. It just stopped, with no notice, no working toward it, no growing apart. So, what does one do?

"You're doing it," my therapist tells me again.

"Uh ok, I feel like I'm just surviving, though. Is that all I'm supposed to be doing?"

"For now," she says.

"Forever," I think.

Grief is always there. Always. He doesn't have a form, yet he is unmistakable. And always he is right beside me, handcuffed to me. I can feel the pull on my wrist. He is always with me. He is always talking to me. Sometimes we have a decent conversation.

"Remember when?" he says. "Wasn't that nice when?"

Most of the time, grief is annoying:

"See that there? Dan's not here to see it."

"Oh, look! Dan would like that, but you can't get it for him because he's not here."

"He is missing this. He would love that, but he's not here."

"You can't do that because he's not here."

All day long he says these things to me. Taunting me.

One of Grief's favorite things to do is wake me up around 3:00 AM. I call it "The Worry Hour". Grief lays beside me, in that big empty spot, now reserved just for him. And he reminds me of my worries.

"The house is so quiet, too quiet. Is India ok? Maybe we should go check on her. Where's the damn cat? We should definitely check on that. Are you sure you locked the door? What about tomorrow? Are we going to make it through tomorrow? Is it going to be a hard day or a normal day? You know it's never normal now, 'cause I'm here. You know you really need to get a job, right? That death money isn't going to last forever. Why aren't you asleep? You are never going to get through the day if you don't get enough sleep!"

Sometimes he changes size, but his form is always the same. On good days he is small and sits on my shoulder like a conscience in a cartoon. On those days he likes to whisper in my ear, "You can't do this, it's too hard!" and I flick him off with a "YES, I CAN. I HAVE NO CHOICE!" But he always flies right back. I spend the day flicking him away, telling him I'm going to make it.

On bad days, Grief rushes and flows until it is a giant mass towering over me. I am so afraid that I huddle in a ball. Words are coming out of his mouth and the pressure of those words push me to the floor. You can't understand his words. They are so big and so loud that all you can hear is a roar of noises. But I know what they are. I know what he's saying.

"HE'S DEAD HE'S DEAD HE'S DEAD HE'S DEAD HE'S DEAD HE'S DEAD HE'S DEAD."

One day, I got an email from Jill. She was looking at pictures of Dan and it was making her cry. She said, "I'm going to look at the pictures of Dan anyway, and remember that he is dead because you have to remember every minute." Wait, there's an option? Some people don't have to remember every minute, every second, that Dan is dead? I guess that's true. She can go about most of her day, and most of her life, and not think about Dan being dead. With that said, I'm sure she thinks about it plenty, because she misses him too. She's not me, though. She's not India. Her life wasn't completely and utterly entwined with Dan's. She can take breaks from this harsh reality. It isn't right in front of her eyes every single second like it is ours.

I have had friends tell me that they would start to text or call him and then they would remember that he is not there, and their hearts would sink. I never did that. I don't get to forget, even for a second, that Dan is dead.

There is no deciding what day you want to sink into nothingness and what day you don't. You don't get up in the morning and say, "I'm just not going to think about Dan being dead today! I'm going to make rainbows and lollipops today!" It doesn't work like that. The grief is always with you. It's just that some days, you can keep moving. Some days you can't. There's no accurate way to tell which kind of a day it is going to be.

It's hard to explain to people how hard grief is by just saying it's hard. Hard doesn't even begin to cover it, but there seems to be no word that does. It is more like every day I have been carrying an invisible backpack. It is full of my grief which weighs one thousand pounds. India has her own one-thousand-pound invisible backpack, full of her grief. She cannot possibly carry a one-thousand-pound backpack. She can't even lift it off the ground. It is too enormous for her. So, I carry it for her. That's what mommies do; we carry our child's things. I carry both of our backpacks, a full ton of grief, for every single second of every single day.

Sometimes people may see me cry and think to themselves, "Oh, she must be grieving right now. It must be so hard when that grief comes up." They don't realize that it is always there. It doesn't go away just because you don't see it. What they see is only a glimmer. I have taken one pound out of my backpack and shown it to you. People don't realize that when I am happy, when I have fun, when I laugh, I am doing it while running uphill as fast as I can with two-thousand pounds on my shoulders. That's how hard grief is. Every day.

The first year after Dan died, I had zero appetite. I didn't lose any weight though. I told my friends that I must be doing this grieving thing wrong. People with extreme grief always lose weight. Couldn't I get anything good out of this deal? I guess the difference is that they stopped eating, and I didn't. I still ate, but I ate because I knew that's what I was supposed to do, not because I cared if I ate or not. I ate because I had no choice, I had to keep going, so I had to eat. Food had absolutely no taste. None. It's not that food tasted bad to me or sounded bad, it's more that it didn't taste good or sound good. I was indifferent to food. It was just nothing, just empty, just there. Food was tasteless, and I didn't care. My husband just died. Why the hell would I care about food?

It took over a year for me to notice that some foods tasted pretty good. However, noticing that it had taste isn't the same as caring about eating it. I don't remember when I started caring about food again. Honestly, I still might not. Some days, I definitely don't give a rat's ass about food.

Buying milk is the worst. Dan's not here to drink it, so I don't need to buy as much, although India still drinks milk like nobody's business. If I buy my usual two gallons, she will take longer to drink it, and I'll have to go to the store fewer times. But maybe she won't drink it quickly enough, and it will go bad? What do I do? I stare at milk, in the milk aisle, in the middle of the busy grocery store. I freeze. I don't know what to do. How much milk should I buy? I can't figure it out. Then my ears start whooshing, and all the ambient noise is blurring together. Then I bite my lip to try to keep my tears in. Then my brain is screaming, "He's dead! He's dead! He's dead!" Then I feel like I need to sit on the floor. Sometimes I do, in the middle of the store. I sit on the floor and try to take deep breaths. That's what they tell you to do when you panic; take deep breaths. I wonder if the people that tell you this realize how hard it actually is to do in the moment.

Sometimes it's not as bad, and I can take deep breaths as I walk away, forgetting the milk entirely. A few times I left my cart in the middle of the store, sat in my car, and cried.

When you go shopping and your husband's dead, every aisle can cause a panic attack. Every aisle is a decision about what you should or should not buy now. Every item on the shelf is a reminder of what he liked or didn't like. Pretty soon you are going through the store as fast as you can, just trying to get out of there before the terror hits. You're dreading the checkout line, because you will have to talk to somebody, and you might lose it. You would be amazed how often things like families come up in small talk at the grocery store. And saying "my husband is dead" is always awkward for strangers.

I lay in bed with India beside me. She can't sleep either, because her dad died in the middle of the night. The second night after Dan died, she took a bunch of her stuffed animals and piled them up in Dan's spot on the bed. Then she squeezed into the middle and I lay on my side. It was clear immediately that she would not be going back into her bed for a long time. We slept like this for 8 months. Every time we changed the sheets, we had to pile the stuffed animals back onto Daddy's spot. Once, I put them all away while she was at school. She came home and put them all back, without saying a word.

A couple of times I mentioned to her that I knew she put them there to save Daddy's spot, so no one else would sleep in Daddy's spot. She looked at me and said, "No! I just want my animals there." Even sleeping next to me, it took at least two hours for her to fall asleep. Then it took hours after that for me to fall asleep.

Sleeplessness and exhaustion were a never-ending cycle. I was just as exhausted when I woke up in the morning as I was when I went to bed the night before. It didn't matter if I went to bed at 8:00 PM or 3:00 AM. When India and I woke up, I was the same amount of exhausted. Many times, I was so tired that I would fall asleep at 8:00 PM when I put India to bed, but then I would wake up at midnight or 3:00 AM and lie awake for hours thinking, "Dan's dead. Dan's dead."

I would think about the night he died. It played as an endless loop in my head. I couldn't think about the future, because there was none. Sometimes I thought about the past, about all the happy memories we had. Grief is a funny thing though. It tends to be all encompassing. It likes to push out all those happy memories, because all the room in your head is filled with the reminders that he is dead. I think it's just trying to convince you that it's true.

I wanted to sleep for months and months, yet when given the opportunity to take a nap, I couldn't. It was more than just being tired. In November, I would say that I wished I could go to sleep and wake up in March. Then all this holiday stuff would be over, and I wouldn't have to face it without Dan. In April, I would say that I wished I could fall asleep and wake up in September. Then I wouldn't have to deal with India's birthday or mine, or summer vacation, or our wedding anniversary. I guess I thought I could survive from September to November. It didn't matter how much I wanted to sleep, though. No sleep came.

For a while, my besties were on sleep duty. They took turns being awake in the middle of the night, in case I needed to text them. I would send a group text at 3:00 AM and say, "Hey did you hear? Dan's still dead." Someone was always there to respond, usually with a smart-ass comment to make me laugh. I didn't realize until much later that they had worked it all out. I just assumed they were up at 3:00 AM for no reason, like me. Turns out that, no, that was only me. They had a reason: they were watching out for me. They were taking care of me.

I laid on the floor a lot after Dan died. Just sprawled out. On the floor. When the grief was too consuming, or life was too hard, I would stop in my tracks and lie on the floor. If the dishes looked too huge, or I noticed his keys on the hook, or if I wanted to cry, I would have this huge need to lie on the floor. If my besties were around, which they were a lot, they would say, "Do it," and they would sit with me while I laid on the floor. If my sisters were around, which they were a lot, they would say, "Why are we on the floor?" as they came and laid next to me. I usually said something like "Why not?" as I laid on the floor and cried. India would just ignore her crazy Mommy.

I needed to lie on the floor. The un-vacuumed, dirty, stained, rough carpet that was my floor is where I wanted to be. It had to be the floor. I never really thought about why that was, exactly, until now. The couch, a bed, or a chair wouldn't do. Those were too "up". They were still living; they were still a part of the world. Not the floor. Nothing happens on the floor. Everything stops. You are not expected to carry on a conversation on the floor. You don't have to hold in tears on the floor. You don't have to move. You don't have to do. Everything stops when you lie on the floor. It was a good place to be.

I did this regularly after Dan died. Usually I was able to keep it in my own house, but sometimes I would go to the bathroom at my in-laws or my dad's, just so I could lie on the floor. The first Thanksgiving without Dan, I spent a long time on my dad's bathroom floor. Occasionally, I ended up on the floor of a store. Oddly, no one ever asked me what I was doing or if I was okay. Several times a day I would just stop and lie on the floor. When we were living with Dan's parents, I would lie on their floor. The floor in their living room that has plush clean carpet, where, when Dan was alive and we visited his parents, he would build fires in the fireplace just for the fun of a cozy fire on a cold night. Their floor is the one where Dan and India wrestled while we all sat around and laughed at the preschooler in footie jammies and a tutu beating up her Daddy.

My favorite spot to lie on the floor was in "that" spot. You see, Dan died in that house, on that floor, in "that" spot. I know exactly where it was. I know exactly at which angle he was lying when he died. That's a memory that will never go away. I used to lie in that spot. I wanted to be where he was in his last moments. I guess I was trying to feel closer to him. All his clothes in the closet wouldn't do. The bed we slept in next to each other wouldn't do. I had to be in that spot. I also laid in the spot on our bedroom floor, next to the bed, where Dan laid before the paramedics came. I felt closer to him lying in those spots, the last spots he ever touched. Part of me wished, or hoped, or thought that if I could just lie in that spot, maybe his body would magically appear there. Maybe his arms would wrap themselves around me, and he would whisper in my ear, "It's all right Jennifer. I'm here. I'm here." Maybe if I stayed in the spot where he died, maybe, maybe something. I don't know what, exactly. Maybe I would break the curse and we could go back to happily ever after.

Everything is wrong here. Everything is different. Nothing is right. Nothing works properly. Nothing is the same. I live in the same town my family moved to when I was eight years old. I would know it blindfolded, but now it is all wrong. Nobody gets that. They all say, "No, Jenny, it's the same town it always was. Nothing has changed." But it has. Everything has changed. It is like living in the rainforest and then waking up in the desert. People tell you it's the same, because it is to them, but you know it's wrong. You know it turned into a desert overnight, that all the water that made it lush and green and beautiful suddenly dried up.

I used to be a wife. I still am, but he's not here. I used to be madly in love. I still am, but my lover is not here. I used to live in a fairy tale, but now it feels like a nightmare. I used to be super mom, but now I can barely get my child fed. So, who am I? A wife, but not a wife. A mom, but not the one I used to be. I don't know who I am, I don't know what to do. The one person who could help me figure it out is dead. He was everything to me. The whole world could fall away, but if we still had the three of us, it wouldn't matter.

What do you do when everything falls away? Survive, I guess. I am trying to survive, and I feel like I'm drowning. I put every particle of energy I have into helping my daughter survive, and I feel like I'm drowning. Everyone says I'm doing so great. I'm "coping" so well, and I feel like I'm drowning. I don't know what to do. I want to be happy, but don't know how without Dan.

I had one more dream about Dan. I was getting ready for bed, walking around the house, checking doors, closing curtains. I stopped in front of the TV to see what was happening in my show. I heard the front door opening and Dan came walking in. He put his wallet and keys down, as if he was just getting home from work.

Then he was standing beside me, watching the last few moments of my show with me. I looked at him and said, "What are you doing home? You're not supposed to be home yet." He smiled.

"Shhh! I left work early. Don't tell anyone." In my dream, India, who was asleep, woke up and was calling for me. I sighed, and was about to go to her when Dan kissed me on the side of the head and said, "I've got this one." Then he walked down the hallway into the bedroom. I got ready for bed, and I could hear Dan singing to India in the background. That was a good dream. That was a good life.

CHAPTER 9:

It Feels Easier to Just Swim Down

∞ ∞ ∞

I don't know how to live in this world, if these are the choices, if everything just gets stripped away.
— *Buffy the Vampire Slayer*

Here's an awful truth about grief: I blame Dan for dying. My rational logical brain knows perfectly well it wasn't his fault. It wasn't anybody's fault. It just happened. It was a bizarre accident.

"What the fuck, Dan?" I say in my head all the time. "I can't believe you did this to me." I feel like he did this to me, like this is all his fault. I blame him for everything. If I have a bad day, it's his fault. If India has a bad day, it's his fault. If something breaks, it's his fault. If something goes wrong, it's his fault. We never ever fought before, and now I blame everything on him. I stub my toe? His fault. I clearly wouldn't have stubbed my toe if I wasn't walking there to do something that he should be doing. I'm stuck in traffic? His fault. I wouldn't be stuck in traffic if I wasn't driving home from counseling, which I only do because he up and died on me. I fight with India over her doing her homework. This, too, is his fault. He was the homework helper, and if he were here, they would quietly be working on her homework together. I'm so mad at him.

It's his fault. He died, and he left me here all alone. He abandoned me. I feel like he abandoned me.

I don't know why I do that. I know that he didn't abandon me on purpose. I know he didn't want to die. I know he would have stayed here if given any choice in the matter. But still I blame him. He's a good scapegoat, because he is dead. I think that's what human beings do. There has to be an explanation, a reason, a why, a person to blame. I have none of those things, so I blame the dead guy who's not here to argue back or make me see sense. This life makes no sense. Dan would be fine with it not making sense, Dan could accept things that don't make sense. I cannot.

I have never been angrier in my entire life than I have been in the three years since Dan died. I am furious at him. Every time I think about him, I have a strong urge to punch him in the face. That is the first thing I will do when I finally get up to heaven to see him. I picture myself walking up to him as he comes to greet me with his arms wide open. I will punch him in the face, then I will kiss him all over, bury my head in his neck and never ever let go for the rest of eternity. He will be okay with it. I'll bet he knows he deserves it.

People don't understand how I can be so angry at Dan for dying. How can anyone be angry at Dan, especially his wife who loved him so much? Maybe it's because I did love him so much. Maybe it's because I fully understand what was lost, more than anyone else. I am so angry I don't know where to begin. I'm angry that he died. I'm angry that he left us here all alone. I'm angry that God let him die. I'm angry that the paramedics didn't save him. I'm angry that I'm stuck here without him. I'm angry that I have to be the responsible one. I'm angry that it seems like he got out of a lot by dying. All the hard work is left to me.

Sometimes I want to scream, "Why didn't you try harder? If you really loved us, like you claimed you did, you would have tried harder to stay here!" I have heard so many stories of people dying who fought to stay. They fought until their family could say goodbye. They fought for hours as the paramedics did CPR, because there was still a chance. They fought with their dying breath to tell their wives they loved them, one last time. I didn't get any of that with Dan.

One reason I'm so angry is because if I'm not angry, I will be so sad I won't be able to function. Being angry at Dan helps me get up in the morning.

"Well Dan, you're not here to get India off to school, so I guess I have to do it myself."

"Well Dan, you're not going to help fix up the house, so I guess I have to do it myself."

The anger keeps the sad away. I'm sure it's not the best coping mechanism, but it's what I'm doing. If I let the sad in, I will crumble. I will fall. I will be so sad that I won't be able to move. I have channeled much of my pain into anger, only letting the real pain out in very tiny slips. I can't afford to do otherwise, because somebody must keep our lives together, and it has to be me. I need to yell at my dead husband every single day. I need to move. I need to keep going. I have a daughter that needs me to get up every day. If I let the sad in, I won't be able to. Maybe someday I will find the time to just lie down and let all the sadness come, but right now I need to keep going. So, for now, I stay angry at Dan.

India and I went to the river with some cousins. India loves to swim. Her Daddy taught her to swim. He was a lifeguard in high school, and it was important to him that she could swim well. She does; I don't worry (much) about her swimming. We had a fantastic time at the river. We swam and swam, we rode inner tubes, and we caught crawfish. Through it all, I missed Dan, and wished he was there, but we were still having fun. You do both. You have to, to survive. Then India saw some other kids, jumping off the side of a cliff. Dan was a daredevil in the extreme, and the giant part of India that is exactly like him said, "I'm going to do that." She knew I wasn't about to jump off the side of that cliff, so she convinced my sister to do it with her. I didn't get a picture because I was too busy being terrified. It wasn't overly high; about as high as a diving board, which she has done many times. Still, it was rocks and cliffs, rivers and danger, and my heart pounded in my chest as she said, "One, two, three, GO!"

She did it. She loved it. She did it again. I'm sure she would have done it a dozen more times if it hadn't been time to go home. It was awesome. Dan should have been there to do that with her. He would have convinced her to jump from even higher up, and I would have been shaking my head at the pair of them.

It's times like these that I flip him off. Sometimes I do it mentally, sometimes physically, and If I'm in the car, I give his ashes the bird. If I'm at home, I will flip off any one of the hundreds of pictures of him that are on our walls. Why do I do that? It's a little passive aggressive to flip off the dead guy you're in love with. Simple answer: I'm fucking pissed as hell at him. I yell at him more now than I ever did in the nineteen years we were together.

I have had several friends tell me that I'm "stuck in the anger phase". I have had several others say that they don't understand why I'm mad at him, because of course he didn't want to die. I know, and it doesn't matter. I know, with my entire being, that Dan would have stayed here with us if he had a choice. That has nothing to do with me being mad at him. I'm mad at him because he's not here, and I am. I'm mad at him because I don't get to sleep in anymore. I'm mad at him because I have to go to school plays without him. I'm mad at him because he doesn't help with bedtime anymore. I'm mad at him because I can't talk to him anymore. I'm mad at him because I don't want to do this nasty life business without him. I'm mad at him because I miss him, and I want him here with me. Unfortunately, that's not an option. So, I have to settle for flipping him off while I watch his daredevil daughter jump off a cliff.

Rage goes well with anger, don't you think? I have rage like I have never known. I truly didn't think it was in me. Death brings out all sides of you, I guess. I want to throw things and kick and scream like India does. I want to stamp my foot with clenched fists and yell up at the sky. I am a grown up. I shouldn't want to do those things. Sometimes I do it anyway. Sometimes I want the whole world to see my rage, so that they know I still feel this loss. I still feel his love missing from me. I think I might feel better if other people would rage like I did. Then I could see their love pouring out in their rage as well. How can anyone expect me to not rage? It is the only thing I think I have ever raged about, and they don't know what to do with me. I'm completely out of character these days. My old character left with my husband, died with my true love. How can I be expected to be the same? I will never be the same.

Throughout our marriage, I would open our bathroom cabinet to get out the toothpaste or hairbrush and see two bottles of seizure medication in two different strengths. Often, Dan would pass behind me to reach them, his hand always seeming to land on my backside, just for a moment, letting me know he was still there, and still found me irresistible after all these years. From time to time he would complain about his pills.

"This is ridiculous. I should stop taking these. I don't need them. I haven't had a seizure in years."

I would roll my eyes at him and say, "Just take them already." Or, if I was feeling like a smart ass, I would say, "Fine! Call the doctor and make an appointment to start weaning off of them." We both knew that the procrastinator in him would never get around to it.

Then he died, and seventeen years of medication had failed us. He left, but those bottles of pills were still in our cupboard. Every day they were staring me in the eye, taunting me. I couldn't stand to look at them. I wanted to scream, "You didn't work! Why didn't you work? You should have worked!" I wanted to smash them into bits.

"So, smash them then," my therapist said. "It would probably help get a lot of anger out." Umm, okay. I guess I will.

Round One: I took the bottles of pills outside to our picnic table. I opened them and spread some out. I got the biggest hammer we had, and I started hitting them. The problem was that seizure pills come in little tiny capsules, and when I hit the table with the hammer, it made the table vibrate and the pills bounced everywhere. The second problem was that I had, and have, terrible hand eye coordination and terrible aim. I wasn't hitting any pills. I was just making them bounce around and spill onto the ground. After a few minutes, I stopped and picked them all back up. This was frustrating. This did not help with my rage.

Round Two: I got out the baseball bat. It was much bigger than a hammer, so I could hit more pills at once. I definitely hit more pills, but the non-smashed ones were still bouncing onto the ground. Furthermore, I wasn't used to swinging a bat and the vibration from hitting the table made my arms and hands hurt.

Round Three: I put both bottles on the table. All I had to do was smash the bottles and all the pills inside would smash, too. It took a few tries, but the bottles did smash up pretty well when hit with a baseball bat. There were still loose pills bouncing all over, so I picked up the hammer again and started attacking them one by one. I also started crying hard, and yelling at Dan, "Why, Dan? Why? Why did you die, Dan? Why?" over and over and over through blurry eyes as I hit at the table with the hammer. I wasn't even aiming for pills anymore.

Then I stopped. The anger didn't feel gone, but I felt tired, like I couldn't go on anymore. I was sad and lonely. I wanted Dan to wrap his arms around me and hold me as we sat on the ground. Instead, I sat on the ground beside the picnic table by myself and cried.

Sometimes I can't hold the sadness in with anger anymore. When I read Dan's writing, it's impossible to hold the sadness at bay. He wanted to save the world, and most of the people that knew him thought he had a fighting chance at doing so. If anyone could do it, he could. I'm sad because his life was cut too short to do more. I'm sad for what the world lost.

Then I read things he wrote to me. He loved me. He loved me more than I ever thought anyone could, or ever would. Dan Stults thought I was the most amazing thing that had ever walked this earth. I never knew why he thought it, and I don't know why I am so special, but I never had a single doubt that he thought I was. I'm sad for me, for our love that is gone, and that I'm no longer his treasured princess. That is how he always treated me, and I miss it.

I read the things he wrote about India. You can tell in one sentence how much he adored her. I used to watch his eyes light up every time she walked into the room. I am sad for her that she has to grow up without her Daddy who loved her more than life itself. I'm sad that he won't be there for her when she needs him.

My heart is sad. It's breaking all over again, shattering into a million pieces. The pain is unbearable. This is why I cling to the anger; it's easier than being sad. I crumple up into a ball on our couch where I was reading his notes. I think I'll stay here forever, until he comes and gets me.

Most of the time I live my life with a dull ache in my heart. Grief is physical; your body can deal with it better than your mind can. Sometimes the dull ache turns into a sudden stab, as if your heart is being ripped from your chest.

Nothing is easy any more. Nothing is effortless. I can't do things I used to. Grief makes you physically exhausted. Not "I worked all day and then took care of my kids" exhausted. It's not the same. This is a whole different level of exhaustion. It's the weight of grief. I walk slower. I move slower. Physical activity of any kind wipes me out. Groceries feel overwhelmingly heavy. Lifting boxes is hard. The grief makes everything else too heavy. The grief weighs more than any box.

I feel so much older than 38. Friends and family ask why I'm so tired.

I reply, "I'm 68. Why shouldn't I be tired? I'm old."

They look at me strangely and say, "You're not 68; you are only 38. You're not old."

I continue, "Are you sure? Because I am a widow and I think the average age for a widow is 65, so I must be at least that old. I feel that old."

They laugh because they think I'm teasing. I do feel old, much older than I should. It is not because I'm lazy or out of shape. It is because my whole entire body is trying to cope, and that takes immense physical and mental energy.

> *I never knew grief would feel so much like fear.*
> — C.S. Lewis

C.S. Lewis got it. Read his book, *A Grief Observed*. I never knew grief would feel like fear. I knew of sadness, and maybe some anger. I was so naive before. I knew nothing of fear. Everything I was afraid of in The Before was ridiculous in comparison. I thought it was fear, but it was the kiddie roller coaster of fear, one curve and a tiny hill. Grief fear is like riding the shooting rocket roller coaster that goes upside down five times and makes you puke. Since Dan died, I am afraid of everything.

I'm afraid my father-in-law is going to trip over India's shoes and fall and break a hip. I'm afraid he will just up and stop breathing like his son did.

I'm afraid my mother-in-law will get in a plane crash and die. Although she's taken that same trip hundreds of times, the last time she flew was on the twelfth of the month, and the twelfth is when Dan died. I was terrified her plane was going to crash because bad things happen on the twelfth.

My dad had a scope in his stomach because he wasn't feeling well. He called me with the results. My brain said, "Cancer. He has cancer. My dad is going to die. I can't do this again." Dad has ulcers. Basically, he's fine.

My friend Mari called and said, "So, I have some news!" Again, my brain said, "Cancer. She's about to tell me she has cancer. She's going to die." Instead she said, "I'm pregnant." I am afraid everyone I love is going to die. I know that happens now. If the person you love most can just up and die, with no rhyme or reason, everyone else can too.

It's not just fear of death. It's fear of everything, even little things. I'm afraid to go out. What if something happens to India while I'm gone? I'm afraid to talk to people I don't know. What if they ask about my husband, and I have to explain that he's dead? I'm afraid to run to the store, what if something sets me off and I start crying in the middle of the store AGAIN? If people call me at a strange hour, I'm afraid they have bad news. If India's school calls me, I'm afraid they're going to tell me something awful happened and she's on the way to the hospital. I never used to be afraid, not like this. I would worry a little. I'm a natural worrier, but not like this. I was never like this. It's because of grief. The unimaginable happened: Dan died. And now that I know it can happen, I'm afraid it will happen all the time. I'm afraid all the time.

I told this to my therapist. She said, "Of course you are. You have PTSD. It makes perfect sense." That did make me feel a little better. You see, I like to consider myself a smart, rational human being. I have Post Traumatic Stress Disorder; people in war get it, people who have been abused get it, and people with trauma get it.

PTSD is the feeling you have when you are afraid of something that you know perfectly well is not going to happen. You shouldn't be afraid of it but are anyway, and you can't stop being afraid. It leads to one of my least favorite things: panic attacks.

I had never had a panic attack before Dan died. If I'm being perfectly honest, I didn't understand them, or the people having them. Don't hate me, but I really truly thought that people who had panic attacks just couldn't get their act together. Since I always had my act together, I had very little empathy for them. After all, what on earth does going out to coffee have to do with your trauma? Everything. It has everything to do with it. Everything is affected. I have learned that now.

A basic panic attack for me looks like this:

Life will be going okay. Not great, just okay. I'm dealing and getting through the day. I am not doing anything "grief related", like therapy or writing. I can be driving, at the store, at India's school, or just sitting on my couch. Then something happens. I see a scene of a seizure on TV, or I see something at the store that reminds me of Dan, or I see a fire truck with its lights on. There are hundreds of possible triggers. It's nothing big, usually. Most people wouldn't even notice the trigger. Sometimes, even I don't consciously notice it.

My heart starts racing. It's beating so fast I can feel it. The thoughts in my head begin to swirl together and get confused. I hear a loud rushing in my ears, like a waterfall or white noise. There is too much noise, but I can't differentiate it; it's like I'm in a bar, with chairs scraping, glasses clinking, and everyone around me talking. Suddenly, I can't remember what I am doing. If I am in the store looking at the shelf full of milk, I won't remember that I was about to pick one up and put it in my basket. If I'm looking at my phone, I won't remember who I was about to call. And the worst part, always, are the flashbacks where I see Dan dying. Dan is dying all over again in my head while I'm trying to buy milk, and I cannot function. I get it now. I understand panic attacks. I only had to go through a huge trauma to have some empathy. I would have preferred to continue living life in ignorant bliss.

For a while, India was in an after-school program one day a week. I took her to school and said, in front of her teacher, "Remember, you have your after-school program today." India said she would remember, and her teacher commented on how fun the program was. They both knew where she was supposed to go when the bell rang.

After school, I got a phone call from the program. They said, "We have India marked absent today." Oh no. India should be there; did she forget and get on the bus? The lady on the phone doesn't know. She's not actually at the school; she just makes the phone calls. Panic panic panic panic panic. My ears are rushing with noise. What if something happened, where is she? My heart starts racing. I am 99% certain that India forgot and got on the bus. But that 1% is screaming that I know bad things happen now. That something could be terribly wrong. That 1% is winning over the 99%. That's what happens now. That's what life is like when you no longer feel safe, when you are afraid. Even if 99% of your brain knows that you are overreacting, 1% will still win.

"Okay, I'll call the school," I say, trying not to sound panicked. But I was panicking.

I call the school secretary and say, "India isn't in the after-school program. Can you ask her teacher if she forgot and got on the bus?" I wonder if she can hear the terror in my voice, as I wait for her to check with the teacher. I'm trying hard to stay calm. I'm trying to listen to the 99% of my brain and not the 1%. It's nearly impossible. Because my husband, who was not sick or injured; died, just died, right in front of me. The chances of that are even less than 1% and it happened anyway. And now my brain is constantly reminding me that bad things can, and do, happen. Not to those other people over there, but to everyone, to us, to me. The secretary gets back on the line and tells me that the teacher can't remember if she got on the bus or not.

"Okay," I say as calmly as I can. "I'm sure she just got on the bus. The bus will be here in five minutes, so I will call you back and let you know if she's on it."

What the hell was I thinking? I can't just sit here for five minutes when I don't know where my child is. It is two days before the two-year anniversary of Dan's death. My anxiety is already high. Perhaps on a different day I would have reacted better, but not today.

"She's on the bus. She's got to be on the bus," I tell myself. No, I can't wait. I start looking up the number to the bus barn to see if they can get ahold of the bus driver to ask if India is on the bus. My hands are shaking so much that my phone won't stay still. I can't think.

The bus barn. I want to call the bus barn. How do I find that number? I don't know. What bus does she ride? I can't remember. Please be okay, please be okay. Calm down Jenny, you're overreacting. Am I? I know I am, but what if I'm not? I can't make it stop. As I'm looking for the number, the bus pulls up, and India jumps off.

"I forgot to go to the after-school program, Mommy." Huh. Yes, Mommy knows all about it. I take deep breaths. She's okay; she was on the bus. See 1%? You lose. I call the school back and tell them she was on the bus, so that they don't worry either.

Half an hour passes, and I'm still frazzled. I can't think. I can't concentrate. She's fine, why do I still feel like I'm in panic mode? This feeling won't go away, my heart won't stop racing, my mind keeps thinking of what could have happened, while telling me to calm down. She's fine. We go to Grandma's. I tell Grandma what happened. She looks at me concerned; she can see I'm still afraid.

"She's okay," Grandma tells me.

"I know," I reply. I go into the bedroom and lie on the bed until dinner, trying to calm my brain down, trying to calm my body down, thinking about my dead husband, because that is always there, too.

Another time, we went to a restaurant with Dan's family. The last time I was at that restaurant was when Dan, India, and I went fishing. The last time India was there was with Dan, his dad, and his brother, right before Thanksgiving. Dan had a seizure in that restaurant. Then they went home, I came and got him, and we went to the ER. That was the beginning of this nightmare. I was kind of surprised his family still wanted to eat there. We sat down at a table, and I started freaking out. I kept picturing Dan having a seizure in the restaurant, even though I wasn't there when he had it. It felt like, if I just turned my head, I would see the whole thing out of the corner of my eye. I breathed deeply, kept my head down, and ate. I answered very few questions. I was concentrating on not having a panic attack.

When we first got to the restaurant, India casually commented that the last time she was here, it was with Daddy. As soon as we got done eating, India said, "Mommy, I want to go home. I want to go home right now." I thought she sounded a little panicked herself, but I wondered if I was reading into it. We left as quickly as we could. As we were getting in the car, India said, "We shouldn't have come here, Mommy. We should have stayed home." Don't worry baby, we will never come here again.

We live out in the country. The only thing out there, besides houses, is India's little country school. We don't even have any apartment complexes; we have farms. One morning I was turning off our road onto the highway to go to the store. Two police cars zoomed by, lights flashing, sirens blaring. The logical conclusion is that there was a car accident. I continued down the highway. Three more police cars zoomed by with lights and sirens. I kept driving. Two more police cars with lights and sirens.

Then it gets fun, because my widow brain started talking.

"What are all those police doing out here? There's nothing out there. The only thing that warrants that many police out there is India's school."

THREE MORE police cars drove by.

"Oh my God. Something happened at school. There was a shooting or a fire. Something's wrong! I need to go to the school!" my widow brain is telling me, as my heart starts to race.

"No, you're being paranoid," my regular brain is trying to say. "I don't know what's going on, but the school is fine. India is fine." I call Mari. She is the voice of reason. She will talk me down. The second she says hello I say, panicked, "I need you to talk me down. I just saw like 9 police cars zoom by toward the school. I need you to tell me that's not where they were going, that everything is fine. Tell me that I'm being crazy and panicking for no reason and that I should not turn around and go to the school."

"Turn around and go to the school," Mari says. Wait, that's not the voice of reason I was expecting. "Do it! It will give you peace of mind," she says. But by now I'm on a part of the highway that is separated by a barrier. I have to drive several miles before I can turn around. She stays on the phone with me as I wipe tears out of my eyes so I can see.

"I didn't used to be like this, you know," I sob.

"I know."

"I used to be a very calm and practical person."

"I know," she says.

"This is all Dan's fault; he made me this way. I didn't used to be this way."

"I know."

"What is wrong with me?"

"Nothing," she says.

When I got to the school there wasn't a police car in sight. There weren't children panicking. There weren't flames coming out of the building. There were no sounds of gun blasts. All was calm, all was bright. I wiped my tears again. Mari was right: it gave me peace of mind. My baby girl was all right. I never found out what all those police cars were for, but it wasn't my daughter's school.

I look in the mirror and I feel tired. I look tired too, but I emanate a feeling of constant tired. Like an aura surrounding me. An aura of tiredness. That's all that's left. The joy is gone. The light in my eyes is gone. That "red headed spark" I was known for has vanished. My magic is gone. All that's left is tired. I get up every morning and my mother in law asks if I slept well because I look so tired. I slept as well as I always do now, which isn't well at all. I'm always tired. I see my friends and they tell me I look tired, that I'm working too hard. Yes, I'm working twice as hard now. Or ten times as hard. You must account for the grief, not just simply the missing person. I go to therapy and she tells me I look tired, she tells me to practice self-care. I try. I'm still tired. No amount of rest, or sleep, or fancy massages is going to cure my tiredness.

I see lines on my face, and my cheeks are hollow. I've lost no physical weight. It just sank off my cheeks and down my jaw and absorbed into other parts of my body, leaving my face narrow and sad. It is no longer round and giggly. I have lines around my eyes, but they are not the laugh lines I am supposed to be acquiring at this age as I watch my small children be adorable. They are tired lines, they are I-don't-know-how-I-can-make-it-one-more-day lines. There is a whole row of them coming out of the corner of my eye. Those lines didn't used to be there, they only showed up after Dan died. They are my grief lines.

I have what I call crazy widow hair. My hair is unruly and wild. I can put it in a tight ponytail or bun every morning, and within an hour it's falling out and going everywhere and looking like I didn't brush it at all. I make no attempts to fix it, I'm too tired to care. It's just crazy widow hair, perhaps it is my emotions escaping through my hair.

I have a fantasy that Dan is in the other side of the mirror, in another world that I can't get to. He sees my aura of tired and he grimaces. He looks sad. He knows it's his fault I am like this and he can't stand the thought that he hurt me in any way.

"You're tired, Jennifer," his lips say.

"I know," I reply. "I can't fix it."

"I can," he says. He reaches through the mirror and grabs my hand, gently like I'm a princess and he's taken my hand for a dance. Just his touch lifts some of the tiredness from my soul. He leads me the rest of the way through the mirror. He leads me to our room and lays me in our bed.

"You need to rest," he says.

"It doesn't work," I say through tears. "I can't rest. No matter what I do, I can't rest."

"I know. I'm going to fix it." He crawls into bed next to me and holds me. I can feel his breath on my neck. I can feel his chest rising and falling. I can hear his heartbeat. His heart is beating, he is alive. He is taking calm deep breaths, trying to restore my soul. I'm crying, but it's working. With every breath we take in unison a piece of my tiredness lifts and floats away. I can feel myself being restored. I can feel my "red headed spark" coming back. I can feel my magic restoring. All we're doing is holding each other and breathing.

That's all I need, and it's the one thing I can't have because it's all on the other side of the mirror. It's all just a dream. It can't really happen.

CHAPTER 10:

Talk less. Smile more.

∞ ∞ ∞

Nobody knows how to handle the 34-year-old widow with the seven-year-old child. It's like a circus freak show, or a *Ripley's Believe It or Not*. No one has ever seen such a thing. Funny, since there's thousands and thousands of us in the U.S. alone. Like an oddity, people tend to stare and then turn away when you notice them looking at you. People truly don't know what to do. It's not necessarily their fault, it's Western culture. We have been taught to look on the bright side of life, and only talk about the good things, so no one knows what to say about the bad.

Pretending my dead husband isn't dead does not help anything. I know he's dead, whether you want to acknowledge it or not. If you think you're doing it for my benefit you are lying to yourself. You are doing it because you are uncomfortable. It does not benefit me in the slightest to have you ignore Dan. If he were alive, you wouldn't ignore him. You would talk about him, you would ask me about him. To a widow there's not much difference. To this widow, not acknowledging Dan or his absence feels as though you don't care, and I'm pretty sure you do care.

People think widows are contagious, like leprosy in ancient times or AIDS in the eighties. If you touch me, I will spread my dead husband germs. It feels as if I'm walking down a hall and people keep turning the other way, not daring to touch me, talk to me, or even look at me because they might catch my dead husband disease. The behavior is most prevalent among my own peer group: happily married moms with small kids. They don't know how to handle it and it's isolating. It scares them to think that it could have been them, but it means that most of the women I know are weird around me.

I got the most weirdness from other moms at India's school. They weren't mean, but they had no clue what to do with me. They couldn't fathom being me. They couldn't imagine being in their 30's and having their husbands die and still getting their kids to school. Neither could I, but here I was. So, they stopped talking to me in the halls, they stopped making light conversation in the copy room. They weren't trying to be unkind; they just did not know what to do. They were afraid of saying the wrong thing, so they said nothing.

I have not met a single widow or grieving person (and I've met lots in this new life) that appreciates a platitude. Please, just don't. I would rather tell you about the night my husband died than to hear you say something like, "When God closes one door, He always opens another." That's not in the Bible, and it's not helpful. Let's pretend for a minute that your friend's spouse died suddenly. You're sad and shocked. You know they are grieving so you try to say something encouraging. Here is a brief list of phrases you might want to stay away from:

- You are still so young.
- Maybe she can marry the new pastor. (Said the day after my husband died.)
- He is in a better place now.

- God needed another angel.
- It hurts me to look at you because it reminds me that he is dead.
- He would want you to be happy.
- It's God's will.
- You have your memories.
- You're lucky you knew to get counseling.
- You had a love like that. Most people never do.
- You're so strong.
- He's watching over you.
- He's always with you.
- Everything happens for a reason.
- I can't even imagine.
- I could never go through that.
- Time heals all wounds.
- You'll find someone new.
- Children are so resilient.
- You have life insurance, that's just like winning the lottery.
- You need to move on.
- It's just like my divorce.

These were all things that were actually said to me. Not a single one of these phrases made me feel better about my situation. They did all get the evil eye from me and rants to my besties about them. Please, for the love of God, do not say any of these things. Just don't. Most of them will make the griever feel worse. Their heart has been ripped out of their chest and shattered into a million pieces, so being told that their spouse is in a better place doesn't help. Can you imagine? I know it hurts, but can you please try?

Your soul mate just died, and you are frantically wondering if any of those things you've seen in the movies to bring people back to life would actually work, and someone tells you that they are in a better place. So now on top of everything, you feel guilty for being selfish and not caring that they are in a better place because you just want them back with you so badly that you wish there was such a thing as vampires.

My husband dying on me is not the same as you getting a divorce. Yes, it's hard, but it is not the same. Your divorced spouse is still alive. Your kids still have both parents in some form.

Your dog dying is not the same as my husband dying. Just don't. Pets are fantastic; I've had some die on me too. Really, it's not the same, I promise.

Do not tell me I am strong. I don't want to be strong, I want someone to be strong for me.

Don't tell me I am brave, what a pile of shit. I am afraid of everything now, I know fear like I have never known before.

Don't tell me this is my opportunity to go back to school. I don't want to go back to school. If I did, I would have done it while my husband was alive so he could have supported me through it.

Don't tell me I can do anything I want. That's not true. I want to be married to my husband and I can't do that. I don't want anything else.

Don't tell me I can start over. I don't want to start over. I loved my life, why would I want to start all over?

Don't tell me you could never do what I'm doing. You don't know. You don't understand that your heart keeps beating no matter how badly it's broken. Days keep going forward no matter how much you want them to stop. You could do what I do, if it was forced upon you like it was me. I would have said I couldn't do it either in The Before, but now I know. You just do it. You have no choice.

We did receive a small amount of life insurance. I went to pick it up from my insurance agent, an old family friend. He said, "Well, I'm about to make your day really happy!" In that moment, a part of my brain acknowledged that money would help us survive until I get a job, and that's good. The rest of my brain screamed, "I don't give a fuckity-fuck-fuck about your stupid money. It's not going to make me happy. It's not going to change anything. And it's for damn sure not going to bring Dan back. So, what the hell is the point without Dan?" I want to tear that check up and throw it at him. I don't want stupid money, I want Dan. Money cannot bring Dan back.

A year after Dan died, someone asked me what was new.

I said, "Well, Dan's still dead." She said that wasn't actually new.

"It still feels new to me," I replied.

She said, "That's why I just pretend it never happened!"

I'm glad she has that luxury. So, I said, "Yeah, well, you don't have to live in my house," which ended the conversation.

I have had people tell me that they that they blocked me from their Facebook feed because all my posts about Dan make them too sad, and they don't want to think about it.

I had someone tell me that it hurts them every time they look at India's face, or mine, because it reminds them of Dan. I have to look at both of our faces every day.

Two of Dan's best friends didn't come to his funeral, they said it was too hard for them. They wanted to remember Dan how he was. I said it was nice they could do that, because I couldn't.

My brother in law wrote a post on Facebook: "2016, worst year ever." I, mostly joking, commented, "Who died?" He replied, "Carrie Fisher." Oh. I hadn't heard about that yet. He was also referring to the slew of 80's stars who died that year. George Michael, David Bowie, Gene Wilder, Prince. Carrie Fisher, however, seemed to top them all. People were devastated by her death. A true princess was gone.

My mother-in-law was slightly offended. To her, 2015 was the worst year ever. 2015 is when her son died. I wholeheartedly agree with her. 2015 is when my soulmate died, there is no worse year than that. There is no comparing that to anything. Of course, that's not what my brother-in-law intended. 2015 broke his heart, too. He was just saying 2016 also sucked. Well, yes, and here I may offend people, mostly because I am a selfish human being.

I am not affected by Carrie Fisher's death. Or the death of any other icon that died that year. Don't get me wrong. I am a child of the 80's, and I grew up watching Star Wars, just like you. Possibly more so, because my dad managed a movie theater my whole life. I spent all my free time hanging out there, watching movies, talking movies. Movies are in my blood. I had the poster from Labyrinth on my bedroom wall for at least three years. They were great actors and musicians. I know their songs. I love their movies. Carrie Fisher was a great role model.

But I never met her, I never talked to her, and I didn't see her every day. I don't have funny stories to tell about her or "remember when's" with her in them. She is not the father of my child. I hear she died, and I think, "Huh. That's too bad," and then I continue with my life. 99% of the population continued with their lives after they heard Carrie Fisher died. Only for her family and friends did life really stop.

When Dan died my life stopped. His parents' lives stopped. Our family's lives stopped. I wondered how the world could possibly go on moving when such a great soul had died. It affected every second of my life. Every single second. It still does. Carrie Fisher's death only affected one second of my life. If you never met Dan, chances are his death did not affect you the way it does me. His death did not affect Carrie Fisher or her family at all. That's okay. They didn't know him. You didn't know him. I don't think anyone knew him the way I did. I wish you had, because he was an extraordinary human being. He didn't have any news coverage. That's okay too. He would have hated all the attention.

Some of you are reading this because you have had your own life-stopping grief. I'm sorry that I never knew your person. I'm sorry that their death didn't make my life stop like it did yours. But I know what it's like for the world to stop, just like yours did. I can imagine how Carrie Fisher's family are feeling about her loss. How their hearts have been ripped from their chests and shredded to pieces. You may be the biggest Carrie Fisher fan in the world, and you may be sadder than I am over her loss. It may affect you for days, or weeks, or months. But chances are, she wasn't a part of the small world that you came home to everyday.

My small world I came home to everyday, that I felt 100% safe and secure with, that I shared my entire life with, is gone. For me that is a bigger loss than the greatest of movie stars. Three years later, it is still as big and all-consuming as it was when it first happened. Dan was my person. Chances are, if you're reading this, you have a loss like that, too. Chances are it's not Carrie Fisher. No offense, Carrie Fisher. You are a fantastic actress and I adore you. Rest in peace.

Sometimes I play the dead husband card. As in, "Well, you know my husband died, so it would be great if you could help me out with this thing." I try not to use it too much. I don't want pity, but sometimes I need some help.

The dead husband card does get you things. It gets you free drinks at Dutch Brothers when they hear you are going to the beach to spread your dead husband's ashes. It gets your freezer stocked with food you did not make for about six months. It gets you lots of looks. Lots and lots of looks. It gets your daughter toys and candy. More toys than a child needs, and more candy than the two of us can possibly eat. It gets you extra moving help when you suddenly get kicked out of your house. It gets your friends' husbands to move heavy things for you and fix broken things.

I don't want to over use my dead husband card. I don't want people to start getting annoyed and saying, "She uses that excuse all the time." I try to take care of India and myself with minimal help from our friends; I try to make do with the same amount of help we had when Dan was alive. Only, here's the rub: he's not alive. In case you didn't hear, Dan died. Those two words make life a million times harder than it used to be. Dan died. Our world is not the same. We do need extra help. I'm still trying to figure out how to do life without him. Sometimes people just throw me the card without me mentioning it. They bring me coffee, they say take a break and rest. They invite India to spend the night at their house so I can have a night off. I love those people.

Sometimes all the little things add up, and you just don't want to do it anymore. You don't want to do anything. Sometimes it's the hundredth time India has called your name in the last hour, and you have to resist the urge to yell, "Ask your dad to help you!" You know that won't go over well. Sometimes, it's when you get phone call after phone call about things you need to do before you can buy a house. Sometimes it's when you can't find what you're looking for at the grocery store. These things make you want to scream, "BUT MY HUSBAND IS DEAD! DON'T I DESERVE A BREAK?" Shouldn't everything just work out now? Shouldn't life be easier? Can't someone just hand me the milk, so I don't have to wander through the whole store looking for it? I must have paid my dues to get an easy life, with this dead husband thing. Shouldn't I automatically win the lottery even though I don't play? Why doesn't my dead husband card work for that? Shouldn't I have gotten an easy life card to play along with my dead husband card? Instead, I got a "life is even harder now" card to play with the dead husband card.

Nobody wants these cards and I have both. How is that fair? It's way worse than getting dealt the old maid.

Then, my best friend came up with an amazing idea. She said I needed dead husband business cards. We laughed and laughed about how I needed dead husband cards that I could hand out to people, and then walk away without having to say anything. How convenient! I could give them to receptionists, store clerks, people that ask me if my husband can help me unload the car when I get home, moms at school. Really, they are good for any number of things. I could even give them to friends when they start acting as if they've forgotten or they think I should be "better by now". Just hand them a card as a little reminder and walk away.

A few days later, I got a package in the mail. It was a stack of 500 professional business cards. Sleek and simple, they said:

> *Smile and nod at me.*
> *My husband died on January 12, 2015.*
> *I'm sorry if I'm awkward.*
> *Thank you for your patience and understanding.*

It's different, and it might weird some people out. But they are so awesome. More importantly, they are a good laugh, at least for me. That's what you do when you're 34 and your husband dies. You cry, you scream, you shake your fists at God, you flip off your dead husband, you are seriously sad and seriously depressed, and you laugh. You have to. If you can't find some way to laugh, you will never make it. I highly recommend all widows get some of these cards.

I took a grief class once, and we were asked what it felt like to be the uninvited guest at a party. I wrote this little story about a witch. I think it's a good metaphor for how I feel, and how things are not always as they appear.

"She can make people vanish," they whisper. "They are here one moment and gone the next, and nobody knows what happened." She can hear them. She is old and frail, but she still has perfect hearing. "She has a black cat that can turn into a panther."

Really, the stuff people come up with, she thinks, as she smiles and nods her head slowly. Nobody nods back. Nobody smiles back. Some try to act like they didn't see her, but they did. After all, by now the whole kingdom knows who she is. They know to stay away from her. They know she wasn't really invited to this party. People like her are bad luck, they carry curses. She stands next to them, but they do not include her. They notice her. How can you not notice her? But they are afraid to talk to her. What if just by standing near her, she can make you vanish? Or worse yet, if you talk to her, she will make your loved one vanish, and then you will be like her: old, frail, and ALONE.

She appears as one would expect an old witch to appear. Long, brittle gray hair, a skinny pointy nose, wrinkles on her face. Not little ones, but big giant wrinkles, almost like folds in her skin. A testament to the cruel life she has had. Her eyes are sunken so deep that you can hardly see them, the color has drained out of them and they look black and empty. She has tried to dress decently for the occasion, but to others' standards it is a disgrace. She has on a black underdress, very plain, something to cover her body. Over that she has layer upon layer upon layer of shawls, all shades of black and gray, some ragged and torn. Rags! How dare she come to a party like this in rags? She does not belong here. She carries, in one hand, a knotted curvy walking stick. On her other hand, her left hand, she has a ring. People say it is a magic ring, that it carries all of her power.

The king and queen enter the room. Everyone bows. The witch bows, but since she is old and frail, she cannot bow as low as the other subjects. The queen notices the witch and fear strikes her eyes, just for an instant. She composes herself very quickly because she knows that she is queen, and must not show her subjects fear, even though she is very afraid. She whispers to the king, "What do we do?" The king has no answer. He knew this day was coming, he just didn't know it would be so soon. He knows why the witch is really here

The subjects take turns presenting themselves to the king and queen. The last is the witch, because she wasn't on the guest list. As the witch is presented, the queen looks her straight in the eyes. She is the queen, and cannot get away with sideways glances, even to her lowliest subject. In the instant where their eyes meet, a swirl of magic comes out of the witch's ring. Everyone turns to glass. The only people awake in the grand ballroom are the queen and the witch. The queen is transfixed on the witch, and as she watches she sees the witch unfold.

First, her layers of shawls come off. The queen realizes that they are not dirty old rags, but that each shawl is a layer of love that surrounded the witch and kept her safe. When you look at them through the eyes of love, they are not black or gray but a rainbow of beautiful colors. Then her eyes come into focus,

137

they are no longer empty and black, but blue and full of happiness and cheer. There is a beautiful fire in her eyes.

"Just like mine," thinks the queen, as they lock eyes with each other. The wrinkles on her face lessen, getting smaller and smaller. They are not wrinkles at all now, just faint lines where it is clear she has smiled too much, it is obvious that once she knew joy. Her hair has turned from gray and brittle to a vivacious red; thick and healthy and falling at her shoulders in waves. Her nose is still skinny but now it looks regal and refined. Her plain black dress swirls about her, becoming a white ball gown covered in diamonds, grand enough for the queen herself to wear. Finally, the crooked staff rounds itself into an elegant crown, silver, also covered in diamonds.

The queen glances at the witch's ring, but she already knows what it looks like. It is the same ring she has on her left hand. A princess cut diamond, with three smaller princess cut stones going halfway around it. The middle is also a diamond, the two outside ones rubies. Indeed, it is even the same hand. They are identical to each other in every way. And the queen knows. She knows.

This is why the witch is here. This is what the queen is to become. It was never supposed to be this way and yet here it is, happening right in front of her. There is nothing the queen can do to stop it. She screams in despair. Her scream breaks all the glass, freezing the subjects. In a sudden rush the ballroom comes back to life. Everyone acts as if nothing has happened. The queen is still standing in the front of her room. The witch and the King have vanished. The queen picks up a shawl left behind and wraps it around herself.

CHAPTER 11:

Death Doesn't Discriminate Between the Sinners and the Saints

∞ ∞ ∞

This is the chapter that will get the most criticism and make people mad. This chapter is about God. God is a tricky subject, because everyone has their own beliefs and almost everyone thinks they are right and everyone else is wrong. That's not why I'm here. I'm here to tell you about my experience with God when Dan died.

One of Dan's favorite quotes was from the movie *Braveheart*.

> *The good Lord told me He could get me out of this, but you're fucked.*

The good Lord got Dan out of this. He is kicking it in heaven. I, on the other hand, am fucked.

I can't think of a better way to say this other than that Dan and I were "all in" on this whole God thing. It's what we did, it was who we were. We went to Bible College because we wanted to learn about God. Dan went to seminary and was working on his Master's in Divinity when he died. We weren't casual churchgoers. We were the ones that showed up early and stayed late. We taught Sunday school and youth group. I helped in the nursery. We went to conferences and on mission trips. We went to all the extra functions. Dan was an elder. We served communion. India was a candle lighter. I can't say we knew everyone, but everyone knew us. It was our life: we didn't do sports, we did God.

Dan had faith like no one I've ever known, while I tended to worry about everything, he never did. He was always saying things like, "God's got it under control." And "It will be fine. God's got it." And "Don't worry, Jennifer. God will take care of it." Dan also prayed a lot. He was one of those people that would not just pray but actually "talk" to God. I was always more practical. I believe in God, but I want a clear answer, a neon sign telling me what to do. Dan had faith. Dan had enough faith for both of us. Many times, it was Dan's faith that got me through. Dan believed God would take care of it and I believed in Dan's faith, so I believed God would take care of it, because Dan told me He would.

We were also what I like to call smart Christians. We didn't think that our belief in Jesus meant that our lives would be perfect. We didn't believe that God would bless us with wealth if we prayed hard enough, although that would have been cool. We also knew that God doesn't necessarily answer every prayer with a yes. We studied, we prayed, we read the Bible, and I always thought we had a good understanding of God.

Then Dan died. Worse, I feel like God let Dan die and I just can't understand why.

"Please God, please God, please fix Dan. Please God, please God, please fix Dan." That was the only prayer I could muster as Dan lay dying in front of me. I said it over and over and over. I could have been whispering or screaming at the top of my lungs, I don't remember. I don't know if anyone else could understand what I was saying as I was choking on tears.

It was a lousy prayer. It was not eloquent in the least. It didn't praise God for His goodness or greatness first. It didn't say let Your will be done. I didn't say it humbly. It wasn't a prayer I memorized in Sunday school. It didn't follow any of the guidelines or rules I was taught about how to pray correctly. Nonetheless, it was the most powerful, important, meaningful prayer I've ever prayed in my life. I can assure you that I have never prayed harder.

Dan still died. Dead forever. God did not answer my prayer. I know God doesn't answer every prayer, but this one was kind of huge. I don't know what to make of that. I don't know why God decided to let Dan die. I'm sure Dan knows, and I don't really think that's very fair, because I want to know, too. I feel like God just stood by and let Dan die.

I always believed prayer worked. I have seen it work. When I was in the hospital, in premature labor with India, Dan prayed and prayed. Dan prayed harder than he ever had in his life that India and I would be okay. It worked. Dan's prayer worked, and we were fine in the end. I want to make a bet with Dan. I want to compare his praying on that day to my praying on the day he died. I want to know who prayed harder, whose prayer was more heartfelt and sincere. You know what? I already know the answer. It is a tie. Both of those prayers were the most genuine prayers either of us have ever prayed. Why, then, did it turn out like that? Why did India and I come out perfectly healthy from that ordeal and Dan came out dead?

My religious education tells me it doesn't work like that. God doesn't answer prayers based on who prayed harder. God has the bigger picture and I don't. That sort of pisses me off, because my shattered heart knows that I prayed the most important prayer of my life, and it's not fair. My heart wants a concrete answer for why my prayer didn't work. I suppose you could give me a very Christianized answer: God did fix Dan. He fixed him in the ultimate way by bringing Dan to heaven. I call BS. I want a real answer. I want to know why.

A friend said once that Dan was one of very few people that actually "walked the walk". That was Dan, true to the core. An actual, really good person right here in the 21st century. All he wanted to do was help people (and get tattoos). Dan wanted to save everyone and everything; he wanted to save the world, the animals, the environment, all of it. It was his life's mission to help people. He wanted nothing but to show people God's love (and get tattoos). He was good at it. He was making a difference. He helped hundreds of people, and he could have helped thousands if he had only had enough time. Why would God let that die? Why would God let such a force for Him die?

I was so mad at God when Dan died that I really didn't want to talk to Him. Dan was leading a life for God, why did this happen? However, I didn't want that for India. I didn't want India to be mad at God. A little mad was okay, but I didn't want her to be so mad she stopped talking to Him. I didn't want her to lose her relationship with God because I was pissed off. So, I prayed with her at night anyway, just like we had always done, even though my heart wasn't in it. The first night Dan was gone, I prayed as tears ran down my face, "Dear God, please help our hearts to not hurt so bad." That was it. That was all I could muster. That was all I could muster for months. Eventually, I added the sentence, "Help us to remember Daddy and talk about him." Then that was all I could muster. Slowly, I added short things, like "Help us get a good night's sleep and help us have a good day tomorrow." That's all I am up to, three years later. That's all the prayer I can muster. I'm trying to lead by example. Dan would come back from the dead and kill me if I stopped teaching our child about God. Would that work? Because I would do that. I would.

I wouldn't say I lost my faith when Dan died. I believe in God, 100%. I know with absolute certainty that Dan is kicking it in heaven, eating bonbons and watching Oprah, having a much greater time than we are down here. However, my faith has definitely changed. I suppose you could say that I'm lost IN my faith. I still believe in God, but I really don't know what to do with Him right now. I read in some widow book somewhere that it takes about three years for a widow to not be angry at God anymore. I read that pretty shortly after Dan died. Three years. Okay, I can do that. I will wait it out and then I won't be angry at God anymore. Like magic. It's been three years and four months as I type this, and I'm still waiting. I think it may be in the same thought stream as "you will feel better after one year". So, in other words, a total crock of shit.

Dan was dying, I was praying, and God did not intervene. God let Dan die. Just let him die, and it doesn't make any sense. The paramedics were performing CPR and I was begging God to save him, and I believe GOD CHOSE NOT TO. It wasn't like I was asking for a giant miracle, like raising someone from the dead three days later. I was simply asking to let modern medicine work. Everything was in place, and God just needed to let it work. He just needed to let the CPR work. Why didn't God let the paramedics save Dan?

My God, My God why have you forsaken me?

That's what Jesus said as he was dying on the cross. That's how I felt on the night Dan died. I have always felt what one calls God's presence. My entire life I have known that God was with me. Not that night. That night there was fear and terror like I have never known, and God wasn't there with me. I couldn't feel His presence. He wasn't anywhere. He left me that night. If God were standing in front of me right now, I am certain I would punch him in the face while yelling curse words. I want to scream at Him, "You're wrong, God! You're wrong. This was a huge mistake you made, letting Dan die. A huge mistake. Can't you see that God? How can you not see that?" Dan's story was not done. Didn't God know that? He had to know that. He's God.

So yes, I am angry with God. I am bloody pissed. I am furious. FUCK YOU, GOD. Not original, I know, but I think it gets my point across. Sometimes I don't know who I'm angrier at: Dan for having the nerve to die on me or God for letting it happen. Usually, after a debate in my head, I conclude that Dan didn't get a say, and therefore I'm angrier with God. I really have every right to be, in my opinion. I wish I could pour out vengeance and wrath on God. I wish there was a way to relieve this anger. Maybe if I could decimate a town, like God did to Sodom and Gomorrah, I would feel better. I doubt it. God didn't feel better after He did that either. God was sad after that.

I will never understand why God let Dan die, and I think that makes me angriest of all. I know the "scholarly" answer is that because people have free will, sin entered the world, and that's why bad things happen to good people. That's why we have diseases like cancer, and that's why people get seizures, and that's why people die. My scholarly mind knows that God didn't want Dan to die either. But right now, it doesn't help me. I don't understand how God did not save Dan. I understand that we as mere humans can't know God's plans, which sucks by the way. But honestly? Right now, that is not a good enough answer for me. And you know what? That has never been a good enough answer for me.

My friend Jill told me once, "I sort of think there's no purpose in people dying. God doesn't let people die to achieve His plan. People just die. And then He uses that to achieve parts of His plan. Kids (babies!) die of cancer and accidents all the time. I can't imagine telling someone, or truly believing, that it was God's plan instead of part of living in a fallen world. Dan was NOT DONE! That is the BIGGEST BUNCH OF BULLSHIT! Holy crap, Jenny. Dan was not done. He was NOT done. And I don't think God took him. I think God can and will do amazing things in the wake of Dan's death, but

God doesn't take children because they're 'done,' and God didn't take Dan."

I have to wonder at people who say they're not angry at God for their loved one dying. "Good Christians" don't get angry at God because this was God's plan, so I should just accept it? That puts me in a quandary. I definitely consider myself a Christian, and I am definitely angry at God. What am I to do?

Well, here is what I believe: that phrase "good Christians don't get angry at God" is a load of bullshit. It is totally okay that I am angry at God. God created the universe, He can handle some anger from little old me. I know God loves me anyway, even if I'm pissed as hell at Him. I'm sure God can understand why I'm so angry at Him right now, and I'm sure He can take it. I hear He's pretty tough. I can be mad at God. It's okay; I have a big God, I know He will forgive me, and I know He will be there when I figure out how to get over my anger. If you think I should not be angry with God, then your God is too small. He is bigger than that.

I think part of my anger is due to my belief system. Dan is in heaven, anybody that knew Dan knows that for a fact. He is fulfilling his dreams of meeting Jesus, Paul, Josephus, Augustine, St. Francis, Bonhoeffer, Mother Teresa, all the great theologians. I wonder how long it will take him to get to them all? Heaven is awesome; it is so much better than this world. Dan is having a fantastic time, I'm sure.

I don't believe Dan can see us from heaven. I don't believe he is looking down and watching us. Here is another thing I know about heaven: there is no sadness, there is no pain, there are no tears. I'm not even sure he can miss us. If he can, it is nothing like the sense of loss we feel here on earth. Dan doesn't miss me like I miss him. That's why heaven is awesome. Again, Jill had a good answer.

"I don't know if Dan can see you or not. If he can, then I bet he can see the whole picture like God does. Because otherwise, yeah, he would just feel sad and there's none of that in heaven. But maybe he does see you and has an understanding of the whole picture and how you and India will eventually be okay and maybe even awesome in ways you didn't expect. Or maybe he can't see the whole picture, but since he's with God, he maybe feels that all will be right eventually."

I do not believe that Dan is an angel. For me, angels are totally separate beings that God created for heaven. They are not dead people. It's a pet peeve of mine when people refer to Dan as watching over me like an angel. Or when people tell me I have an angel in heaven. Dan is not "with me in spirit" either. His spirit is in heaven and stays there. It doesn't come down here, unfortunately.

I don't believe in signs either. If I see something that reminds me of Dan, I think, "Oh, that reminds me of Dan." I do NOT think Dan sent it to me. Once again, Jill has a good answer.

"I don't think Dan can do anything, but God can. Maybe God sent you something to remind you of Dan." Maybe He did, or maybe it just reminded me of Dan the way everything does, because Dan was such a huge part of my life.

A lot of church has to do with God, but it also has to do with the people, the songs, the memories. All of it involves Dan. We all know I met Dan at church camp when I was 16. From that day on I did not have a single religious experience without Dan. When we sing songs in church, I remember singing the same song in high school, standing next to Dan. When the pastor gives his sermon, I think, "That was funny, Dan would have liked that." Or "You just quoted one of Dan's favorite theologians." Or "Huh. I wonder what Dan would say about that sermon." We would take communion together. He would hold India up as we sang. I think I can count on one hand the number of times I went to church without Dan.

Our church has always been a second family to us. We have always been "core members" of our church. When Dan died, our church was totally crushed. Just like everyone else, they put their arms around me and held me up. They took care of India and me. They were not going to let us fall; they were not going to lose us too. Like my family, they have supported me in everything I've done since Dan died. Before he died, they supported both of us in everything we did. The only thing that changed was the lack of Dan, which of course changed everything.

After Dan died, I didn't know what to do. So, I kept doing everything the way I normally did, as much as I possibly could. I went to church as much as I possibly could. The first time I went to church after Dan died, I was numb. I was still in shock. I went through the day like a robot. All I remember is sitting in my chair crying the entire time. Tears staining my face for an hour and a half. It was okay. Nobody was trying to fix me. They all understood that there was no fixing this. We were sitting with our friends, somewhere in the middle of the church. That's all I remember. I don't even know where India was. It wasn't where we normally sat. We would never sit in our normal seats again. I couldn't do it. Dan was a back-row sitter, always and everywhere, at school and especially at church. It was just his way. He liked trying to go unnoticed, so we sat in the back and off to the side.

At the funeral we had an open casket. I was worried about India and the other children there having to see Dan if they didn't want to. I wanted the kids (and everyone, really) to have the choice to see his body or not. I didn't get that choice, but at least everyone else would. The folks in charge of the building decided that a good place for the viewing was in the back of the church, and off to the side. They moved the chairs there to make room for his casket, the same chairs we always sat in. The irony was not lost on us that the final time he was in church, he was in his usual spot: in the back and off to the side. I guess he was right about it being inconspicuous. India and I never sat in that spot again. It was one of those tiny little things nobody notices but you. One of those things that's no big deal, except that it is. I could not sit there anymore.

As the months went by, it became harder and harder to get myself to church. I wasn't on autopilot anymore; the exhaustion was catching up to me in a harsh way. Sometimes it is just too hard to get to church. I spend all week getting us to the places we absolutely need to go: school and therapy. Everything else is secondary, and that includes church.

I don't believe that you have to go to church every single week or you'll go to hell, but I do think you should go regularly because community is good for your soul. And it's certainly not that I don't want to go to church. It's that I literally do not have enough energy left in me by the end of the week to get India or myself dressed. People tend to think the time in between the death and the funeral are the hardest on a person, but really it's after that. When you are expected to get back to your normal life and you can't because your normal life is dead.

I don't really sing in church anymore. I was never much of a singer anyway, but I always appreciated the words. Now they just make me mad. They say things like how God is in control and how He is watching out for you. All I can think is, "Yeah, but where were You when Dan died?" There are songs about praising God, but I don't want to praise Him. I want to scream and yell at Him. I don't want to sing about His goodness or how He has me in the palm of His hand because for the first time in my life, I don't feel like He does. So, I don't sing. I want to sing. I want to be assured of all those things. I just can't right now.

Often, when I am at church I will have split second flashbacks of Dan's funeral. I will lift my head up from praying and see his wooden casket in the front of the church. I blink and it's gone. It's that quick, but still it was there. I will look out of the corner of my eye, and suddenly the place is packed like it was at Dan's funeral. People are standing up against the windows because there are no more seats. I refocus and they are gone. I blink again, and see a friend sitting across from me. She is crying. No, that's from the funeral. I was so thirsty during the funeral. I guess remembering awful terrible things in split seconds like that is part of the PTSD. Often, I will leave and hide out in the nursery. My friend is the nursery worker and she has her own terrible grief story. It is very different than mine, but it is severe trauma and heart ache, so she understands my need to hide. I sit in a rocking chair and look at her.

"Having a day, are you," she says. It's not a question. It's an observation. She gets it.

Everyone at church is concerned about my wellbeing. I went to a meeting at church. It was for the "leaders" of the church. I'm not exactly sure why I went, because I'm not exactly a leader. I used to be. Dan and I used to be, but not anymore. I'm lucky if I get there once a month now, but I went to this meeting anyway. While there, I mentioned how it was all I could do to get there occasionally, and I was trying.

"I promise I'm trying." They all looked at me stunned.

"We know that, honey. You are doing awesome. You just do what you can, it's fine!" was the group consensus. Then the person leading the discussion added, "While we're on the subject, I just want to tell this church how proud I am of them for all the love and support you have showered on Jenny and her family." Translation: you didn't let her fall after Dan died. You held her up, you carried her. You didn't let her slip through the cracks because she didn't show up every week. Instead, you took care of her.

Many times, I think I can make it to church, but India is a giant mess, so there is no way she is going to make it. She can't stay home with her dad, after all. Many days we even get dressed and are at the point of getting in the car when something happens, and it just gets to be too much. Those somethings are and aren't grief related. For instance, she could stub her toe as she's putting on her shoes and will start crying. It's like opening the floodgates and she can't stop. She will cry and cry and cry. It started because her toe hurt, but it won't stop because she misses her dad so much. This happens a lot with church. The only thing to do is snuggle her until she calms down. It generally always means missing whatever we were going to do. It's okay. I get it. It's too much for her. It's too much for anyone. I do worry that other people don't get it, though, and that they don't understand why we can't get to church. After all, that's how I used to be in The Before. I didn't understand why people couldn't get their acts together enough to show up. I get it now. This was a terrible way to learn that lesson.

One day as we were going to church, India got punched hard in the gut by grief. It had been several months since the last big punch. "You know what, she is doing really well lately," I'd been telling everyone. She had been going to sleep overs, her anxiety had lessened, and she hadn't had a "grief tantrum" in months. She was doing really well.

Then that Sunday came. We were going to church! We were going to make it to church that day. My friend from a neighboring church was going to be there, and I said I would sit with her, and afterward we would go out for lunch. We were going to make it to church!

"Time to get dressed India! We are going to church today!" I said.

"Ok, Mommy!" She got dressed in a timely manner and everything. I guess I should have known something was off. She asked if we could drive through the coffee shop on the way, so she could get a chocolate milkshake and I could get coffee. My parenting in The After is superb. I am highly concerned with the nutritious breakfasts she gets, so I said that of course we could go to the coffee shop. Milkshakes it is. Everyone was happy. I even told the guy taking our order, "We are going to church today!"

About half way to church, India found out that her friend wasn't going to be there.

"I don't want to go anymore, Mommy." I explained to her that we were going to church today, we were already halfway there, and just because our friend can't go is not a good enough reason for us not to go. Then it happened. Grief punched her in the gut. She went into a grief tantrum, and a giant one at that. She started crying and screaming uncontrollably. Crying that she had no friends, crying that I was a mean Mommy, crying that she had no one to play with, crying because she wanted to go home, crying and sobbing uncontrollably. She even said, "I don't know why I'm crying, but I can't stop." Then she did something new and fun. She unbuckled herself and climbed up into the front seat, still sobbing.

"I need snuggles Mommy!" Indeed my poor Baby Girl, but I'm driving right now. We got to church and cried some more in the parking lot. Then she started to calm down, so we went inside. We went straight to a classroom so she could calm down some more before actually going to church. That plan backfired. As soon as we got into the classroom, she started screaming and yelling and throwing things. She was mad. She was pissed at the world. Church was starting. I tried, again, to calm her down, but it was to no avail. She climbed on top of a shelving unit and sobbed and sobbed. And threw things.

"I don't have anyone to play with!" she screamed. I get it. I get it now.

As calmly as I could, I asked, "Would you play with Daddy, if he were here?"

Her voice flew up, and at the top of her lungs she screamed, "I can't play with Daddy anymore!"

Do you get it? Do you get it now? She always used to play with Daddy at church. They would run around and play, while I stood and talked. It was one of her favorite things. Unfortunately, I can't read her mind, but I think her thoughts that day may have gone something like this:

"I am going to run around and play with my friend at church today. Oh, she's not coming, oh well, I will just play with Daddy instead, he's just as good. Oh..."

It only takes that one thought. It only takes one second to have that overwhelming grief punch you in the stomach. No, Daddy won't play with me at church. Daddy will never play with me at church again. Daddy is never coming back. Never. You always know he's dead, but sometimes it hits you in the stomach all over again and you can't breathe. When this happens to me, I want to throw up and I usually end up on the ground crying. I want to throw things, but I restrain myself. India is ten. She doesn't care about restraint. She throws things, she screams, she wants her Daddy. Eventually she falls to a heap on the floor, sobbing while I hold onto her shaking body.

Now we are calm enough to go home. There is no chance of us going to church, it's not going to happen. Still crying, but we are calm enough that I can drive. We walk out to the car, and three different people come over and hug me. They could see India's red tear stained face. I have no idea if they know what just happened. I have no idea if they could hear her screaming across the entire church. I have no idea if they knew this was all because of grief, or if they thought I had just taken to beating my child.

At the car, another friend was waiting for me. She was the one I was supposed to sit by and go to lunch with. She gets grief. On the verge of tears, I say, "We just can't ever make it to church anymore."

"You made it to church! You're here! I saw you," she replies.

When India is calm and in a good mood, her remarks on God and heaven are very wise. She got that from Dan. Once, we were snuggling in my bed playing with our cat, Gem. I said that our snuggles were missing a Daddy in them and I wish he could come down from heaven to snuggle.

"When will we see Daddy again?" she asked.

I said, "Not until we go to heaven, which will be a very, very long time from now, when you are a grandma."

India very nonchalantly replied, "But Daddy said that when Jesus comes back, all the people in heaven will come back with him. So, Daddy is coming back."

"Yes, Daddy was right and that will happen, but we don't know when, and I think we will probably go to heaven and see Daddy before Jesus and Daddy come back here." I don't know if she believed my timeline or not, but either way she knows she will see Daddy again eventually.

Sometimes I think India is not worried at all about seeing Dan because she knows she will, eventually. I know I will eventually, too. The difference is that I know how long eventually can last. India doesn't. To her, eventually could be 80 years, or it could be tomorrow. She doesn't know how long 80 years can be.

Once, India was reciting John 3:16. Dan taught it to her when she was three or four.

"Mommy," she said, "it says that whoever believes in Jesus will have eternal life."

"Yes, it does."

"So doesn't Daddy have eternal life then?"

"Yes, but Jesus means eternal life in heaven, so when we die, we don't really die we go and live forever in heaven. That's what Daddy did. He's alive, it's just not down here with us."

"Oh." She went on to tell me how good it was that we believed in Jesus so when we are very old, we can go to heaven and live with Daddy.

Dan wrote a thanksgiving prayer once:

> *For a gracious God whose love endures forever, for the incarnate Christ who invites me to mission and fullness of life, for my wife and closest companion for the last 15 years, for my daughter who brings light and joy to my life, for my parents, who continue to love me, teach me, and support me in so many ways, for my whole family, who have the rare blessing of truly enjoying each other's company, for my wife's family, who bring whole new levels and dimensions of humor, wisdom, and experience, for the country I live in and the freedoms this affords me, for living in the most beautiful part of that country and around those who care enough to protect that beauty, for the home I live in, the heat inside it, the water that flows through its pipes, the food on the table, and the cars in the driveway, for the company I work for who supports doing good in people's lives and my own professional growth, for an amazingly loving, faithful and supportive church community who for some reason seem to really like us, for the greater church community found within our denomination in which I have found tremendous opportunities to serve and amazing mentors, for overall health and the people, tools, and knowledge to maintain that health, for the unending blessings and overflowing goodness which is undeservedly mine, I am thankful.*

CHAPTER 12:

A Mind at Work

∞ ∞ ∞

Dan was a therapist. He was born that way. It was just who he was. He couldn't not help people. In high school, all the girls would ask him about their boy problems, because Dan would sincerely listen and then give great advice. It was who he always was. He wrote this about his passion of being a therapist:

> *I have a passion for children and youth, but added to it is the mentally ill, the disenfranchised, all those who find themselves without a voice in our society. People tend to be at ease around me because I am genuinely interested in understanding them and helping them. Being a counselor is what I am, not just what I do.*

Even though I had never been to therapy, I had a good sense of what therapy was like and what I was looking for from a therapist, because I had learned so much from Dan. Someone told me once that I was so lucky that I had that knowledge. I suppose three years later, I can look back and see how it was "lucky" that I did have some minor background in therapy. Yet I still don't consider it luck. I married Dan because I was head over heels in love with everything about him, except for the paper hoarding and procrastination. Dan was a therapist by nature, and I was in love with that about him, too. And because I liked to hear him talk, I listened and paid attention. I had conversations with him about his work, so I had a basic knowledge of therapy.

I had a therapist within a month of Dan's death. I knew I needed help. There was no way I was getting through this on my own. I found a therapist at an office I was familiar with, because Dan had some acquaintances there. She looked like she would be a good fit for me. For most people, this is the hardest part. I emailed her and told her my story: stay at home mom, dead husband, what the fuck do I do now? Also, you may have known my dead husband; you have mutual friends. She hadn't known Dan, but whatever I said in that email had her convinced that I was definitely messed up, and she said she would see me. I don't remember our first session. I do remember she asked me if I wanted to come back the next week and I vigorously nodded yes.

When I picked my therapist, I went largely off the bio on her website. She had what I needed. I don't remember what that was now, but it was something that I thought would help me deal with my grief. It turned out she is a damn good therapist, and she knew what she was talking about. She tends to tell it like it is, which is something I can appreciate.

I like my therapist. I feel like in another world where I didn't need to go to her for therapy, we could be friends. I also think that is what makes our therapy sessions work. I am comfortable enough around her to tell her how I'm really feeling, to cuss and to cry. I can tell her how I miss Dan so much that it hurts to breathe, and she looks at me with understanding and empathy. I can tell her that I'm an awful mother and she calls me on my BS and tells me why I'm not. I can tell her how I'm so pissed off at Dan that I'm certain when I see him again, I will punch him in the face. She says, "Yeah! Do it!" I tell her I feel like I'm failing, and she tells me to give myself a fucking break. I tell her I'm trying so hard to just survive and she says, "I know." Once, in the nicest way possible, she told me I looked like shit. I felt like shit, so I probably looked like shit too, but to hear your therapist say that means you are having a really hard day.

For the most part, we talk about two things in therapy: my dead husband and my kid. They take up a lot of our time, like they are this huge part of my life or something.

Her opening line is usually, "How are you doing?"

My opening reply is usually, "Dan's still dead," because that pretty much sums up how I am doing. My husband is dead. I'm doing great, life is rainbows and lollipops, except that it's not. So, I opt to tell it like it is. If you are going to do therapy properly, where you actually talk about what is bothering you, and you are willing to explore that with your therapist, it is going to be harsh and it is going to get deep. It is emotional exhaustion like you have never known. I cry more often than not in therapy, and when I don't, I brag to my friends. "Hey, I went to therapy today and didn't cry! Go me!" They are very proud. It's always totally draining, and I don't really do anything afterwards. Sometimes I want to kick and scream all the way there and back like India does, but I can't because I'm driving.

One time I made my therapist cry, by having her listen to an old recording of Dan telling me how much he loved me. This is what Dan said in his calm, cool, slow voice:

> *I promise to love you forever, for always, more than anything, more than anyone, with all my heart I love you. I promise to be the best boyfriend I can be to you, the best fiancé someday that I can be, and someday the best husband that I can be to you. The best father that I can be to the kids that we're gonna have. I promise to always do*

my best to treat you like the queen you deserve to be, like you've always, always deserved to be. To remind you that you are beautiful: beautiful soul, beautiful heart, beautiful face, beautiful body, beautiful you. You will always be beautiful to me and I will always love you. I promise. I promise that someday this time will seem like nothing, when we spend our lives together, I love you girl, don't forget it.

He held true to those promises until the day he died.

Every so often in therapy, we come back around to the night Dan died. I, of course, wish everything had happened differently. I wish I had done this or that. I wish I had called 911 one minute sooner. Maybe that one minute would have made all the difference. I regret being too scared to do CPR when the 911 dispatcher told me to. Maybe if I wasn't so scared, I could have done it, and that would have saved him.

"How do you get past that?" someone once asked me.

"You don't," I said. "You go to lots and lots of therapy and you try to believe your therapist when they tell you, 'You were in complete and utter shock. You were first-hand witnessing the most traumatic thing in your life. It's amazing you could talk on the phone at all. Or even move at all. You have PTSD. You watched your husband die and you have PTSD. Give yourself an effing break.'" She's a good therapist.

I had PTSD. Post-Traumatic Stress Disorder. A disorder that comes after traumatic stress. It is mostly associated with people that have been in war or have been terribly abused. It took me awhile to admit I had PTSD, not because I didn't think I was royally messed up, but because people like me don't get PTSD. Before Dan died, I could easily say that the most traumatic thing that had ever happened to me was giving birth to my daughter. Before that, the most traumatic thing that had ever happened to me was when I was

10, and accidentally spilled a pot of boiling water on my legs. That's it. Three things, and the other two are laughable compared to Dan's death. I had a good life. I've never broken a bone, I've never been in a serious car accident, I was trauma free. But it turns out that watching your husband die is severe trauma.

Whenever I think about the night Dan died, my feet start freezing. My feet would get cold often in The Before. Dan would always tease me about my bad circulation and then get me a pair of fuzzy socks. I distinctly remember having freezing cold feet when Dan died. They were so cold, that in the midst of all the chaos, I had my sister go and get me a pair of socks from my room. She came out with the same fuzzy socks Dan always got me. They were different shades of purple. My feet stayed cold for a month, or more after Dan died. They wouldn't get warm, no matter what I did. They still get cold when I think about Dan dying. When I have a panic attack. When I miss him. When I don't think I'm thinking about him, but I am. When I tell my story. My feet always get cold.

Another thing PTSD does is take your good memories away, so that all you can seem to think of are the bad ones. For instance, I will try to remember a great memory of Dan; we had thousands, even hundreds of thousands. We had 15 years of a great marriage for me to remember. Let's take a memory of him kissing me, for instance. Dan kissed me many times a day, every day. We always ended our night with him kissing me and telling me he loved me. We would lie in bed and he would look at me with his stunning blue eyes. He would lean over to kiss me. Yeah, this is a great memory. Go! Go! Go! STOP! STOP! STOP!

The memory stops and a flash of him dying jumps in its place. It could be of him having his seizure, of the paramedics, the moment I realized he had died, or anything in between. It's like being photo bombed with a giant "HE'S DEAD". It tends to ruin your happy memories.

Make it go away, dear Lord, please make it go away. I can't even begin to try and live with these flashes of Dan dying in my head all the time. Apparently, I have some pretty intense PTSD. How do I make it go away? Did you ever have something embarrassing happen to you and then for days afterward you kept replaying it in your head? Someone making fun of you, or falling in public, or saying something stupid? After a few days, the sting fades, and you stop recalling it. PTSD is exactly that, times a million.

I imagine it's different for everyone, but this is what it was like for me:

The memory of the night Dan died, the awful sickening memory of watching him die, played through my mind 24/7. It was like a video on repeat. It was always there. The whole world was still going on, but that memory was with it. Hold your hand about six inches from your face and spread your fingers out. You can see all around you, but you have this giant hand blocking most of your view. The hand is the PTSD and the images of that night, and they blocked my view of the rest of the world.

Or imagine a transparent screen across your face. You can see what's going on around you, but there is something else, too. You can see what the picture is on the screen, but you can see through it too. On this screen was the night Dan died, over and over and over on repeat. Me pulling his body to the floor, and the fire truck pulling up in front of my house with the lights flashing. Me, trying desperately to hear a heartbeat, opening the door for the paramedics. Equipment, paddles, I can't see what they're doing, someone's in my way. "His heart isn't beating good enough." Good enough? What's not good enough? A heartbeat is a heartbeat. I fall to the floor. I am crying and screaming, and Dan isn't moving.

So, you're driving down the road and you can see what you're doing. You can see the cars in front of you. You can see green lights, and people crossing the road, but you have to look through the screen of this horror movie while you're driving or having a conversation with someone. You can be looking right at them, even talking to them, but the movie is playing in front of your eyes. It's distracting.

At the bottom of your mind is a news ticker. You know the text crawl at the bottom of a news broadcast? On this ticker, it says, "Dan died, he died, he's dead. Dan died, he died, he's dead. Dan died, he died, he's dead." It's the only story on the crawl and it plays over and over and over.

So, to sum up: I had real life, my transparent movie screen playing the death scene, and the ticker tape highlighting the story. Then there's the noise. PTSD brought, for me, lots of ambient noise. It was nothing specific, just noise. It was like being at a busy bar and trying to listen to a conversation, but there was loud music and clinking glasses and 100 other conversations going on around me. There were chairs moving and people dancing.

That was all happening in my brain, while I was trying to get through life; while I was trying to take care of India, make breakfast, pay bills, fold laundry, drive, and see friends. I wasn't really in the world. I was stuck inside my PTSD.

"Have you ever heard of EMDR?" my therapist asked me about six months after Dan died. I had, actually. Dan took a class on it once and talked about it all the time. He had raved about how wonderful it was. I didn't know a lot, just that it was for PTSD and had something to do with following a finger with your eyes. which somehow reprograms your brain. EMDR stands for Eye Movement Desensitization and Reprocessing. My therapist gave me more details, then she gave me the name of a therapist that was trained in EMDR. So, I set up an appointment with her.

Different therapists do EMDR in different ways, but my therapist had me close my eyes, and tell the story of my trauma. It was awful, but I was already replaying that night constantly, so what was one more time? You recall the trauma in sections, but not necessarily in chronological order.

"Tell me about the 911 call," she began.

With my eyes closed, I said, "The clock said 11:15..." Every so often she would stop me, and I would open my eyes. Then she moved her finger around in a funny pattern, and I would follow it with my eyes. Then I would continue with the story, or she would ask me about something I said in the previous set.

"You said your feet were cold. What did that feel like in the rest of your body?"

Sometimes she gave me the next topic while my eyes were closed. "What happened when the paramedics got there?"

This process reprograms your brain. It takes all the memories that are stuck in the front of your brain, and moves them to the back of your brain, to long-term memory. It worked beautifully for me. It took my movie screen, rolled it up, and put it away. It's still in my head; I can get it out if necessary, but it's not in front of everything now. The ticker tape went with it, although it likes to sneak back in often. All the noisy chaos went silent. Now, when I remember that night it's like watching a silent movie. The chaos is gone.

The reprogramming took some time. I needed eight one-hour sessions, but it varies, depending on your trauma. I did it over the summer while I continued going to regular therapy, but some people choose to stop regular therapy while they do EMDR. Doing both can be intense. For me, life was already extremely intense, so what difference did it make?

When I left an EMDR session, it was a strange mix of feelings. On one hand, I was immediately better: my brain was clearer, I could think straighter, I was calmer. On the other hand, I was completely drained and unable to function for the rest of the day. I would go home and try to nap, or just lie on the couch with the TV on.

A year after Dan died, I wasn't feeling any better. In fact, I was feeling worse. The EMDR helped a lot, but I was still a mess. I was utterly exhausted, both physically and mentally. Not "worked a 12-hour day" exhausted. Not even "just had a baby" exhausted. I've done both of those. This was out of the realm of either of those; the English language fails and there is no accurate word for my level of exhaustion.

I had spent the last year trying to survive and trying to help India survive. I went through crying and raging and bedtime. I had to do everything, from getting a glass of water to watching India kick ass in swim lessons, completely by myself. I didn't get to share her achievements with Dan. I also didn't have him to hold me when I was crying so much I couldn't catch my breath. He wasn't lying on the floor beside me when I needed him so badly. I was just barely keeping it together.

Picture an *Indiana Jones* movie. Indy has just got the treasure and is making his big escape. He starts running, and it is one thing after another: first he has to leap over a giant cavern in the ground, then he gets shot at by 50 poisoned arrows, then he has to swing across a ravine on a vine. But wait! That vine is actually a snake's tail. Now he's being chased by a giant rolling boulder, now surrounded by rats, and, oh crap! The room is on fire! He runs and runs and runs. He is running so fast, trying to hold onto his treasure, that he doesn't realize he is at the edge of a cliff. He falls over, and all hope seems lost. He is holding on to the edge of the cliff by his fingernails, but at any second the cliff could give way or his fingernails could break off and he would fall into nothingness. If only somebody would come grab his wrist and pull him up.

That is the first year of grief. I was constantly panicked, constantly afraid, just running and trying to keep my treasure

(India) safe. By the end of the first year, I felt like I was hanging off a cliff by my fingernails, just hoping that someone would come grab my wrist before I fell into nothingness.

I was trying. That's what I kept telling everybody when they would ask me how I was doing. "I'm trying. Really, I'm trying."

Sometimes they would say, "I know you are, honey," and sometimes they would just look at me. Was it pity in their eyes or were they thinking, "Geez, it's been a year already. Why can't she get her act together by now?" Some people would try to convince me I was doing a fantastic job. I would scoff at them. Clearly, they don't see me enough if they think I have anything at all under control. I was trying so hard to hang on. I was working my ass off just trying to survive. I felt like I needed to scream it at everyone that walked past me, "I'M TRYING!" I felt like it was all I could give as an explanation when India missed school, yet again. It was all I could say when people would comment that we needed to eat healthier food, or when they would comment that India's hair wasn't brushed or she didn't have a coat on. "I'M TRYING!" When I was late for something (which is my biggest personal pet peeve and now I do it all the time) or when I said no to helping a friend. When I was too exhausted to get up from the couch, or when all I could do was lie on the floor and cry. "I'M TRYING" was the only excuse I had.

"I know you are," is all my therapist would say about it. "I know you are."

I went to my weekly therapy appointment after the one-year anniversary of Dan's death. I honestly barely remember what was going on around this time. One year, and I was barely functioning. I wasn't better, the way everyone thinks you should be. Where do people even get that shitty idea? I was hanging onto a cliff by my fingernails. It's entirely possible that this was the session when she told me, in the nicest way possible, that I looked like shit. I did look like shit. I also felt like shit.

"I can't do this anymore," I told her. Of course, I've been telling her that since the first time I saw her. I think maybe this time she agreed with me though, because she just looked at me. She said perhaps I could use some more help. She meant drugs, the prescription kind. She referred me to a psychologist who could prescribe me antidepressants, and maybe some sleeping pills. Sleep sounded really nice. Could I sleep until June?

That same week, I saw two of my counselor friends and told them that my therapist was referring me for antidepressants. Both replied with an enthusiastic, "It's about time!" Yes, I agreed. I needed some massive help. At the same time, I was wondering why on earth it took everybody this long to tell me. Why didn't they prescribe antidepressants from the get-go? Didn't they hear the tragic story of my husband's death? Of course I was depressed! Wasn't that a given?

"We wanted to see if you could come out of it on your own," my therapist said.

I had to wait six weeks before there was an available appointment with the psychologist. In the meantime, I kept hanging on to the cliff with my fingernails. As with all new doctors, there were a thousand forms to fill out, with the dreaded single, married, or other boxes to check. Sometimes they have a "widowed" box, but this form didn't. I checked "other" and wrote over the top of it "widowed".

There were several questions pertaining to why I felt I needed a psychological appointment, such as:

Why did you make this appointment? My husband died.

What contributed to this issue? My husband died.

Why do you think you have this issue? My husband died.

When did you first experience this issue? When my husband died.

Next, it wanted to know if I was in a committed relationship. I checked the "yes" box and then wrote next to it, "but he's dead." I should have been able to scrawl over the first page with a giant Sharpie "MY HUSBAND DIED!" and that should have been a sufficient answer for all questions.

I met with Dr. Ava. She knew who Dan was. She had never met him, but she had sent her nursing students to his work. She said she had heard lots of good things about him. Of course, she didn't know the fun details of him dying, so I had to tell her all about that, and that always wears me out. It really is exhausting, telling people over and over how your husband died. I must have convinced her that I needed help, because she immediately prescribed me antidepressants and anti-anxiety medication, which she said would help me sleep.

Take the antidepressants every single day, once a day. The anti-anxiety pills were to be taken before bed. If I didn't fall asleep in an hour, Dr. Ava told me to take another one. I could do that up to three times and I did, often. I could even take them during the day if I felt I needed to. Their purpose was to slow my heart rate, which in turn would calm my anxiety, which in turn would help me sleep. It worked and worked well.

The first time I used them, I could feel my body calming down. I still had trouble sleeping, but the medicine made it about 50% better, which I was more than happy about. Some nights, usually around a holiday or a big event, it felt like the pills did nothing at all. I texted my friends, "The doctor didn't tell me what to do when you've taken all the fancy pills you're allowed and you still can't sleep." I found the answer to that. You stay awake.

A lot of grieving people are afraid of taking antidepressants. They want to feel every second of the pain. They don't want to bury their grief with drugs. I get that. I didn't want to do that either, but I knew that no matter what I did, my pain was not going away on its own. It hurt to breathe. I also knew I couldn't keep going like this. I needed help. Both my therapist and psychologist explained it like this:

It doesn't take your pain away, it just doesn't. It is not magic. It doesn't make your dead husband come back, so it doesn't fix anything. What it does is give you space. It gives you space to breathe, and it gives you space to catch your breath. It sounds cliché, but that is exactly what it did for me. It gave me space to breathe. It gave me enough so that I could take a deep breath before a panic attack would set in, and maybe I could then breathe out of that one panic attack. Sometimes I couldn't, but sometimes I could.

It gave me enough space so that when India was having an anxiety attack, I could stay calm and be with her and not panic myself. It helped me not care about things I didn't need to be wasting energy on, like my house being a mess or my third grader doing her homework. None of that matters when you are just trying to survive.

From time to time, I went to check up with Dr. Ava to get my medication refilled. I mostly just sat there and told her what was going on. It was just like therapy except they took my blood pressure and prescribed medication. Every time I went in, I had to fill out a small survey. It had questions on it like "How often do you wake up in the middle of the night?" Then there were multiple choice answers: All the time; Sometimes; Rarely; Please mark one. My favorite question on the survey was "How often do you think about death or suicide?" I always laughed, because I could see where they were going with this. They wanted to know if you were thinking about committing suicide, but that's not what it asked. So, I circled the word "death", and marked the "all the time" box, every time. I think about Dan's death almost constantly. I don't think these questions were made with widows in mind.

Therapy helped, EMDR helped, and medication helped, but my heart was still shattered. A year and a half after Dan died, I walked into therapy and got my usual, "How are you doing?"

"Dan's still dead," I replied. He's dead, he's dead, he's never coming back, he left me here all alone to do everything, and I'm mad at him. I miss him, and I don't want to do this all by myself, and I want Dan, and this fucking sucks, and it hurts. It hurts so bad, physically. Right now, my entire body hurts. I want to crumple onto the floor. I want to sink into nothingness. I want Dan to hold me. I don't want to do this anymore, but I don't have a choice. I'm still here.

CHAPTER 13:

We'll Bleed and Fight for You

∞ ∞ ∞

India did not handle Dan's death the way anyone expected her to. She certainly didn't handle it the way I expected her to. Of course, I didn't know how she was supposed to react. I've never known anyone whose father died when they were seven. She experienced the biggest trauma of her life thus far, and hopefully it is the biggest trauma she will ever experience. She didn't know how she was supposed to react, either. None of us did. Her Daddy was her hero, and she had him wrapped around her little finger from the second she was conceived.

Dan wrote once:

> *So, I just got done walking with my daughter to the gas station so we could buy junk food. We walked down the road, holding hands, and talking about whatever came our way, which included bugs, string cheese, wind, and caramel popcorn. Oh, and spinny dresses. It was fun. She's cute, and smart. Yeah, I think my kid is the best. She deserves someone who thinks she's the best.*

As India grew, it became obvious that she was a lot more like Dan than like me. I used to say it was a wonder she was mine at all, but Dan would say he could see me in her. He said we had the same facial expressions, but she has always had her Daddy's beautiful eyes. Daddy was her hero. At three years old, he was also her Prince Charming. She loved playing "getting married" with Daddy. I would officiate, and she would wear her fanciest dress. Dan would be all decked out in shorts and a T shirt. One time, when he was buckling her into her car seat, he leaned over and gave her a kiss. I teased him, "Hey, where's my kiss? I want a kiss!" India pointed her finger right at my face and said as sternly as a three-year-old could, "Get your own prince."

Dan and I used to say that India was going to grow up and conquer the world. She could do nothing less; she was just that fun, clever, and headstrong. She was a precocious little daredevil, willing to try everything (except food, she is a picky eater) and not afraid of anything. India was the girl that wanted to swim in the ocean in January, that wanted to hike to the very edge of every cliff. She wanted to climb waterfalls. She was, and is, brave, strong, imaginative, and creative. She is smarter than me, and possibly smarter than her dad. We were raising her to conquer the world.

> Dan: "So, if I didn't buy you a treat, would I still be the best Daddy ever?"
> India: "Well no, but don't worry Dad. I'll always love you even if you're not the best."
> Dan: "Really couldn't ask for anything more, I suppose."

India coped with Dan's death by pushing it all deep down inside. It was like she didn't want to acknowledge that he had ever existed. She refused to talk about him; she refused to even say his name. When I talked about him in front of her, she would instantly change the subject or literally run away; she would spin on her heels and run into the other room. She didn't want to talk about him dying, and she didn't want to talk about when he was alive. She didn't want to talk about him at all.

I didn't understand. I wanted her to be sad like I was. I wanted her to say, "I miss Daddy." I wanted her to say the word Daddy. Just say Daddy. Say you're mad at Daddy, say you miss Daddy, say anything at all! Just talk about Daddy. She wouldn't do it. I would try to encourage her to talk about Daddy by starting conversations about him.

"I was just thinking about Daddy. Do you ever think about Daddy?"

"No. I'm too busy having fun," she says.

"Yeah, but I still think about Daddy, even when we're having fun."

"Stop it, Mommy! Stop it. We are supposed to be playing and I want to play," she says sharply. I back off.

Sometimes she has what I call "grief tantrums". She rages. She kicks, screams, and throws things. She lays on the ground, her face red, her fists clenched, her toes flexed. Her hair is wild around her face as she shakes her head back and forth and beats at the carpet. She will scream at anyone that comes near her. They won't, though; they don't know how to deal with her. I don't know how to deal with her either, but I cannot leave her. She is mine.

Others don't believe that it is what it is; for some reason, they can't see it: visceral, indescribable pain. They can't face that pain, and they think it's inappropriate, so they stay away. They want to go on being appropriate. They don't want to admit that this great injustice, DEATH, is real.

She's only seven. She hasn't learned what is appropriate and what isn't. She hasn't learned the words to say, "I'm sad because I miss Daddy." Why would she know that? What Mommy would think to teach her child how to act appropriately about the sudden death of her Daddy? It doesn't flow easily off the tongue like the ABC's.

She thinks she is all alone. Her eyes are clouded with tears of rage and she can't see anything else. She is not alone. Sitting next to her, lying beside her, is Mommy: the only other person she has seen rage at this great injustice. Everyone else seems to be okay with Daddy dying.

"What is that about?" she wonders, "What is wrong with them?" I hand her another toy.

"Here, throw this one." We rip pieces of paper to shreds. We hit our pillows. She kicks her toys. She stomps through the house, screaming. I follow her. I will not leave her like this; I will not leave her the way she feels Daddy did. She is not alone in this.

She slams the door in my face and I silently wait; I know she didn't mean it. The door opens and she is there, a tiny heap on the floor, crying uncontrollably now. Not raging, just crying. I try to scoop her up in my lap, but she won't let me. So, I push some toys out of the way and lie down beside her. I let her cry. There is nothing else to do. There is no fixing this, and there is no bringing Daddy back. If I stay beside her, at least she knows she is not alone. Mommy is right here.

In the first three years since her daddy died, she has had more grief tantrums than I can count. For a while they happened every day: giant tantrums that you would see in a two or three-year-old, complete with crying, screaming, kicking, and throwing things.

Except she's not two. A two-year-old does that because they haven't learned to focus their emotions and put them into words. Once they learn those skills, they grow out of the tantrums. My daughter has grief tantrums for the same reason. She doesn't know how to put her emotions into words. At seven, eight, and nine years old, she has no words to explain the emotions that come with her Daddy dying. She doesn't know how to focus or control this massive grief. At 37, I don't know how to control my massive grief. How can I expect her to? This isn't a "didn't get her way" tantrum. This isn't a "you won't give me ice cream" tantrum. This is a terrifying "my Daddy is gone, dead, never coming back, and I can't grasp that" tantrum.

For the non-grieving, it can look like she is having an "I didn't get my way" tantrum. It starts as something small and innocuous: she can't find the pink crayon, she doesn't want to go to school, she doesn't want spaghetti for dinner. It's not about that. It's never about that. The pink crayon reminds her of the time she and Daddy drew a garden of pink flowers. Not wanting to go to school is because she's afraid that, if she leaves her side, Mommy will die too. Not wanting spaghetti is because Mommy doesn't make it the way that Daddy used to.

Her therapist explained it very clearly to me once. He said to imagine that you're walking down a road. If somebody bumps you, it's just a little bump. You shake it off and you keep going. But kids who have had trauma are walking on the edge of an emotional cliff. If they get bumped, even a little bit, they are now falling off a cliff.

That describes my daughter exactly. Every little emotional bump is huge to her, and she doesn't know how to handle it. No wonder she's screaming and kicking. Somebody bumped into her and, because she was already on the edge, she's now holding on to a cliff by her fingernails.

The summer after Dan died, we went to visit my two best friends. They both have husbands and kids. We had a good weekend playing with our friends. My daughter ran around in the back yard with the other kids while the dads chased them. She laughed and squealed and had a great time playing with the other kids and their dads. Her dad didn't play with her. She hadn't played with her dad for six months. He was dead, and she could never play with him again.

Sunday morning, we were all going out to breakfast before we started our long drive home. India didn't want to have her hair brushed. We argued back and forth about it for a few minutes, and then she started raging. She had held her grief in all weekend, but she couldn't do it anymore.

Fists clenched, screaming at the top of her lungs, she stomped into the room where we were staying and slammed the door. You could hear her yells throughout the entire house. I went into the bedroom; she had crawled under the bed and into the corner so I couldn't reach her. She didn't want to be comforted. She wanted to rage! She was pissed off that her Daddy wasn't there, and she had every right to be.

I tried to coax her out, "Come on, honey. Let's calm down so we can go to breakfast." She screamed louder. Nothing I could say would calm her down. Finally, I poked my head out the door.

"Why don't you guys go on to breakfast and we will catch up in a little bit."

This made her scream louder. She didn't want her friends to leave, she wanted to go to breakfast with everyone else, she wanted to be normal like everyone else, and she wanted her Daddy just like everyone else. It was never about brushing her hair; that was just how she got pushed off the cliff. She doesn't know how to express this:

"Mommy, I had so much fun with my friends' daddies this weekend. It made me really miss all the fun things I used to do with my Daddy, and that makes me really sad. So, I'm going to cry about Daddy for a little bit. Will you hold me while I do that?"

Eight-year-old children don't talk like that. I mean, she is very intelligent, but most adults can't verbalize those emotions. How can I expect her to?

At seven-and-a-half (the half is a big deal to her), Her parents tucked her into bed every night after reading her a story. We said our prayers together. We sang the "Mommy and Daddy Love You Song", a song Dan made up for her. It ends with all three of us singing, "It just makes your heart so big!"

I kissed her good night and said, "I'll see you in the morning!" Then I walked out of the room.

Dan kissed her goodnight and said, "I'll see you in the morning!" leaving the door opened a crack as he left the room. She didn't see him in the morning. She never saw him again.

Her best friend was GONE. Her playmate was GONE. Her hero was GONE. Her Daddy was GONE.

Before her Daddy died, her biggest worry was whether or not we would be having ice cream for dessert. That should be a seven-year-old's biggest worry. But overnight, her worries went from ice cream to who was going to take care of us, what was going to happen to us, and what if Mommy dies too. She shouldn't have that on her shoulders.

This is what we do. This is how she is handling her grief. Some days, India will rage and cry for over an hour. Once, in the middle of a tantrum, she bit me three times. She hasn't bitten anyone since she was two. It was like you see in movies when someone is in labor and they give her a stick to bite down and on. She was laboring. She needed something to bite, and Mommy was right there.

Right now, India is mad at the world. Right now, she is full of anger and rage. Her dad is dead, and she misses him. That one little fact makes everything, every day harder. Grief makes every single thing harder. It makes breathing harder. It makes putting on a pair of pants harder. It makes facing the world harder. It's no wonder she's so mad at the world; she can barely get her pants on.

India's pain also shows itself through anxiety. After Dan's death, anxiety attacked her like a demon from hell. All of a sudden, she was afraid of everything. She worried about everything. Our daredevil adventurer was now afraid to leave the room without

Mommy. Fear ravaged everything. It was right beside the grief. It was the grief.

I didn't know what to call these attacks she was having, because I had never seen anything like them. Was it anxiety? Was it grief? Was it fear? Was it anger? Was it the deepest, darkest sadness ever faced? It was all of them combined. It needed a name. How do I tell somebody she has anxiety because her dad died and this is part of grieving?

"Yes, I know it was three years ago, but it was just like yesterday for us." That explains it but is also really long. I thought about naming them something like, "My-Effing-Dad-Died-I'll-Fucking-Cry-If-I-Want-To" attacks. That also explains it but would probably get me a lot of looks.

In the end, I just settled with anxiety. My daughter India has anxiety. It started when she was seven because her dad died. If I'm feeling up to it, I may explain to you that it is one of the awful ways that people grieve, but don't get your hopes up. Just know that anxiety sucks and you're lucky if you don't have to worry about it, especially in your little kid.

I was only aware enough to start noticing her anxiety two months after Dan died. Dan's grandmother had just died. Yes, two months after her son died, her mother also died, my poor mother-in-law. India and I were flying by ourselves to Minnesota for the funeral. Dan's parents were already there. We have ridden an airplane several times to Minnesota to see Great Grandma and Grandpa, just not without Dan. I didn't realize how hard that would be for both of us. It had never bothered her before; India was always excited to go on an adventure, and I didn't know yet how much everything relates to grief.

She woke up the day of the plane ride saying her tummy hurt and she didn't want to go to Minnesota after all. She refused to eat breakfast. In the car she kept getting more and more nervous. She said she felt like she was going to throw up. My dad kept asking if he should pull over. At the airport, she started to cry and begged to stay home, but we had to go. We got on the plane. The first leg was a little jumper plane, which was noisy and turbulent. She was so scared that she made herself physically sick. She kept crying and crying that her head and her tummy hurt really, really bad. It was the worst airplane trip we had ever been on. All because of anxiety, which was all because of grief.

When we landed to change planes, I thought that maybe she was actually sick. After all, she had never acted like that on a plane before. I didn't realize yet that grief had given her anxiety. I didn't realize yet that it had given me anxiety either, but it had. I bought her some Tylenol and decongestant from the airport for around five million dollars, give or take. We ate lunch and she was feeling much better.

Then, we got on the next plane and she was nervous and anxious again, saying she didn't feel good. She was so distraught that I didn't know how we were going to make the two-hour plane ride. Finally, I convinced her to climb up in my lap and put her head on my shoulder. She worried herself out and fell asleep on me for 40 minutes. She was better after that, but still nervous when we started to land. On the way home, I had her take some children's Dramamine, in the hopes that she would fall asleep and we could avoid another plane ride like we had on the way there. She didn't fall asleep, but with that, a good movie, and gobs of chocolate, we made it home.

She always has anxiety when she has a substitute teacher or even a substitute bus driver. By always, I mean since her dad died. Before that it didn't faze her at all. She is afraid that having a substitute means there is something wrong with her teacher, and that her teacher could die. That's what she thinks about now. Sick means dying, gone means dead. Once, her teacher was sick for several days, and by the end of the week India's anxiety was so bad she also stayed home from school.

She takes her stuffed animal to school with her every day, hiding him in her backpack. I'm totally fine with her doing so, but it tells me she is feeling insecure at school, which never happened in The Before. One Tuesday, her bus driver informed the kids that they would have a substitute driver for the rest of the week. On Wednesday, she got off the bus and exploded into tears. She was terrified that the driver would miss her stop. She begged me to pick her up for the rest of the week. I tried to calm her down by telling her everything I could think of about the bus system: The sub has a list of all the stops, and he has to check them off as he goes, so he won't miss yours; Mommy is standing in the driveway waiting for you, and she will tell him to stop; You can tell him to stop; The bus turns around and has to pass our house again, so we can make it stop then. She knows all of this. She's a smart kid. But the anxiety won't let her think. When the anxiety is in control, she can't stop it, she's too afraid. I drove her to and from school the rest of the week. I didn't want her to be terrified all day at school and crying all the way home. We have bigger things to worry about, like making it to school in the first place.

She spent years afraid something bad was going to happen. Especially to me. She hated it when I left the house without her. She needed a detailed itinerary of where I was going to be when, and when exactly I would be back. She was terrified that if she let me out of her sight, I would die. I know exactly where it came from. Dan was absolutely fine, kissed her goodnight, and said, "I'll see you in the morning." The next thing she knew I was waking her up and telling her that he had died. Just like that. He didn't keep his promise. He meant to, he wanted to, and he had every intention of doing so, but he didn't, and at 7 (and a half) years old she didn't understand that sometimes adults break promises unintentionally.

What she did understand is that Daddy said he would see her in the morning, and he didn't.

With a child's understanding, why should she trust me when I say, "I'll see you in a couple hours," or "I'll be home for dinner," or "I'll see you after school?" She doesn't fully believe me. There is a little piece of her mind that says, "Yeah? Daddy said that too and look what happened." I can see it in her eyes. What's worse is that there's a little piece of my mind that agrees with her. Life is no longer a sure thing. When Dan and I went to sleep that last night, I was sure I would talk to him in the morning, but I didn't.

She did other things to make sense of Dan's death, and to push it all down where she didn't have to deal with it. They were only things her Mommy and Daddy would notice, but her Daddy was gone, so only I noticed.

When she was two, Dan gave her a teddy bear that had been his as a child. Dan had named it Mic Rac, and he told her how special Mic Rac had been to him, and how India needed to take extra special care of him. Mic Rac was special. He was a doctor of sleepology, and could always help someone fall asleep. He immediately became India's favorite stuffed animal. This was the go-to bear: the one she couldn't go to sleep without, the one that would kiss her good night, the one that went to the doctor and took the shots first to prove how brave he could be. Mic Rac was so special that if we forgot and left him at Grandma's, we would be turning around. Dan used to make Mic Rac talk to India in a funny voice. For being a doctor of sleepology, he wasn't all that smart, and India laughed and laughed at the silly things he would say.

A day or two after Dan died, India put Mic Rac on Dan's side of the bed and has hardly touched him since. For a long time, I thought she might be mad at Mic Rac. I asked her once if she was angry at him, but she said no. I said, "Oh. I just noticed you never really play with him anymore, so I thought maybe you were mad at him or something." She got up, found Mic Rac, kissed him, and put him on the bed. But she didn't play with him. He now sits on her bed by her pillow, and occasionally she will hold him. But he isn't her special animal anymore.

The night Dan died I put India in my bed and that's where she slept, for months and months and months. Somewhere I wrote down that it was eight months. I don't know how accurate that is. It might have been longer. Not only did she start sleeping in my bed, but a plethora of stuffed animals came with her. She laid them all out, in a very Daddy shaped way, on his side of the bed. She slept in the middle and I slept on my side. Every time I changed the sheets, I had to take all the stuffed animals off and put them back on again.

Once, I tried putting them away in her room. She began raging and insisted that we put them back. She carried them, one by one, from her room and put them back on my bed as she cried. I tried to calm her down.

"Okay, baby, okay! We can put the animals back. I know you like them there so that nobody can take Daddy's spot, and that's okay. We can put them back."

At the top of her lungs, she yelled, "I DO NOT! I JUST LIKE THEM THERE!" We put them on the bed anyway. The reason didn't really matter.

There was no sleep to be had in our house, no matter what we did. Dan died in the middle of the night while we were sleeping, so sleeping now seemed impossible. It took an average of two hours for India to fall asleep. We were both exhausted, but we couldn't sleep. I read to her, I sang to her, we laid there in the quiet as she tossed and turned. We would go to bed at 8:00 PM, and I was lucky if she was asleep by 10:00. India was terrified of going to sleep. I think she was afraid that if she fell asleep, I would die too. She slept in my bed right beside me. She could not sleep unless her hands and feet were touching me, and her face was mere inches from mine. When I was pregnant with her, she had a great knack for kicking me in the ribs. I would often express my gratitude that that didn't happen anymore. Only now she was seven and needed to be so close to me that I was once again being kicked in the ribs.

Once I got her to sleep, I had to try getting myself to sleep. I also had problems with that whole "trauma in the middle of the night" thing. Neither one of us were sleeping well, we were both miserably tired, and I didn't have the strength or energy to do anything about it.

Friends and therapists made suggestions. Try some melatonin. Get a sound machine. Here's a great mindfulness book. It all helped a little, but nothing helped completely. I was elated on the nights where it only took an hour for India to fall asleep. Those were the good nights.

One night, we were getting ready for bed, and she said, "I want to sleep in my bed. It's just that I'm scared. I'm scared I will disappear. Things disappear. My old teddy bear disappeared, my favorite jammies disappeared. What if I disappear?"

"Yes," I said. "I totally get that. I'm afraid people will disappear in the middle of the night too, because Daddy disappeared in the middle of the night when you were sleeping. Now I'm scared other people will disappear too, like me or you or Grandma or Grandpa." She quickly changed the subject.

I knew sleep wasn't going to begin to get better, until we were both in our own beds. I started talking to India about sleeping in her own bed.

"I can't, Mommy. There are monsters in my room." Shit. I have no idea how to evict monsters, especially monsters that only took up residence after Daddy died. "They live under my bed and are scary." I didn't think she was really scared of monsters, and in The Before she would have loved having monsters in her room. She would have partied all night with them. I did know she was truly scared to sleep in her room. She had good reason.

We started talking about the monsters in therapy, and ways to deal with them. We decided two things would be the most helpful: magic monster spray to make the monsters go away, and a monster ambassador to negotiate with the monsters on India's behalf. We made spray with pretty smells (monsters hate pretty smells) and lots of glitter (monsters also hate glitter). We sprayed it all over her room, then we sprayed it all over the house for good measure. We did this several times. We also made an ambassador. India drew what she thought he should look like, then she picked out fabric and I sewed him together. His name is Oggedy Boogedy and he's a nice monster. He will tell all the other monsters to leave India alone.

We started having slumber parties in India's room, both of us. Once a week we would both sleep on the air mattress in India's room. Then we upped it to twice a week. Then we upped it to every other day for about a week. Then we both slept in her room on the air mattress for an entire week. Then India slept in her own bed, but I slept on the air mattress in her room for a week. Then I would go in there with her, but after she fell asleep, I would go to my bed. The whole process took several months, but it worked.

The first night she slept in her room by herself, she kept saying she didn't want to and that she was scared. But she climbed in bed anyway, and we hung out for a while. Then she cried a little and said she couldn't do it 'cause she was too scared. I told her that she was right. It was very, very scary, because the last time she slept in her bed was the night that Daddy died, and I understand because I was scared, too. By then we were both crying. She didn't ignore me, and she didn't deny it. She didn't scream or kick or rage. She quietly nodded her head in agreement. It was a huge step for her, to acknowledge those feelings. Then she fell asleep while I was reading.

India was sleeping in her own bed and I was sleeping in mine. It took eight months to get there. It lasted two weeks, and then the new school year started, anxiety reared its ugly head, and she was back in my bed again. It took months for me to work up the energy to go through the process again. It worked. A couple weeks later it was Christmas, and anxiety won again. She slept with me for several more months. This has been our bedtime for the last three years. It takes months to get her to sleep in her own bed, then something stressful happens, like a holiday, and she is back in mine.

On Facebook, Dan posted this:

> Dan: Hey kid, I love you.
> India: I know, Dad, you tell me that every day.
> Dan: And somehow it doesn't feel like it's enough!

I didn't feel that India was coping the way she should be. She was afraid all the time of everything. She didn't want to play with her friends, or even leave the house. This isn't what I wanted for her. This isn't what either of us wanted for her. We wanted her to be brave and strong and fearless. I had to do something. I had to fix our daughter. I couldn't disappoint Dan in this way.

CHAPTER 14:

And You'll Blow Us All Away

∞ ∞ ∞

An invisible barrier separated him from the rest of the world.
— J.K. Rowling, *Harry Potter and the Order of the Phoenix*

India was different now, and everyone knew it. She was the one with the dead Daddy. Her schoolmates looked at her in awe. Grownups looked at her pityingly. Nobody, of course, had a clue what to say to her.

India started with a counseling intern named Mary Beth. Because of Dan's connections, we were hooked up with one pro bono. She was pretty good. India seemed to like her as a person just fine, but she hated going to therapy. India hated everything having to do with Dan's death, and since we only went to therapy because Daddy died, she hated going.

Mary Beth did sand tray therapy with India. This is a type of therapy where you choose whatever you want from a shelf of figurines, placing them however you'd like in a tray of sand. You are supposed to put them in place, without thinking too much about it. Then you tell a story about all the things you placed in that world, and what they are doing. I tried it once, alongside India, and I was amazed at how well it worked; how the items I just thought were pretty helped tell the story of my grief.

Mary Beth told me, "India is very strong willed. She just will not do anything she doesn't want to do." I laughed. It was a good observation, but an understatement. Anyone who talks to India for five seconds will figure that out about her. I knew she was strong willed before she was born.

One day, Mary Beth suggested that I should casually mention to India that Daddy had died because there was something wrong in his brain and that he wasn't sick with a cold or a flu you could catch. She said that even if India was not asking about it, it didn't mean she wasn't thinking about it. This thought had never once entered my mind. Of course I knew that a seizure was not something a person could catch like a cold, but India did NOT know that. She didn't even know what a seizure was.

So, one night while we were watching TV, as casually as I could I told her, "Daddy died because there was something wrong in his brain. It wasn't a sickness like a cold or a flu that you can catch. Mommy can't catch it and India can't catch it. Aunties can't catch it. Grandma can't catch it. Did you know that?"

The look on her face was stunned, as if I had just blown her mind. She responded very calmly, "No, Mommy. I didn't know that." I could tell by her look that she had been wondering if we were going to get sick, too. The poor little thing. How long had she been worrying about that?

We liked Mary Beth. However, she went on maternity leave and decided she didn't want to come back. Her new baby was too adorable to leave or something. She referred us to a lady named Amanda. Amanda was very bubbly. Bubbly is not India's cup of tea. Their personalities did not mesh at all. The rages about going to therapy got worse. I knew Amanda was not the right fit for India, but I didn't know what to do about it. She needed therapy badly. She continually told me she didn't want to go see Amanda. One day, I told India that if she could write me a paragraph with real reasons why she didn't want to go to Amanda any more, I wouldn't make her. She wrote me five sentences scrawled out across four pieces of paper. They were:

Mommy misses Daddy as many grains of sand there are.
India doesn't miss him that much.
I don't like Amanda.
I'd rather stay home and play with my baby kitten.
She doesn't have any good toys.

I didn't know what else to do, but I knew Amanda was a bad fit, so I let her stop going.

My therapist recommended a therapist in her office for India, and I contacted him. I decided to name the new therapist Magic Therapy Dude, or MTD for short. He was going to help India. He was going to be able to get through to her, I just knew it. There was a month or two between stopping with Amanda and starting with MTD when India did not go to therapy. She was having raging tantrums almost every day. One day, she had a grief tantrum that resulted in me saying, "THIS is why you're going back to play therapy!" She was unaware of that. I didn't mean to tell her that way. I was going to tell her when she was in a great mood and make it all exciting and fun. It was not a great parenting moment for me.

I explained to her that her anger and emotional explosions were because, even though she didn't want to talk about it, she missed Daddy and this was how it was coming out.

She screamed, "NO, I DON'T!" and started crying. She told me that her crying was all my fault.

I replied with, "No, it's not my fault that Daddy died." I think she understood, because she was quiet after that. The next week we started seeing MTD.

MTD has lived up to his name. First, he does this funny thing where I go to therapy with her. I sit on the couch and try not to butt in as they interact. I also bring up things that she doesn't want to talk about, like her dead dad. The first time we went to MTD, he tried to get her to label the strength of her feelings on a scale from one to ten.

Do you know what my kid told him, after I spent hours the night before filling out forms describing how anxious and angry she was, and detailing her panic attacks and grief tantrums? A two. Her anger was level two. Her fear and worries were at level two. I had to bite my tongue to avoid butting in. But MTD is very good, and he could see right through her.

MTD did magical things, like talk to her about the monsters in her room, only he replaced the word "monsters" with "worries".

"The worries in your room are big," he said. "You need to sleep with Mommy because you have worries. Oops, I mean monsters, when you don't sleep with her." He is magic.

We also attended the Dougy Center for Grieving Children and Families. It is a support group in Portland for children who have lost a parent or sibling. Essentially, the Dougy Center gives you space. It's a space to talk about your dead parent where kids don't look at you funny because they all have a dead parent, too. It's a space to not talk about your dead parent if you don't want to, and nobody says anything about that either. It's space to play with other kids like you; just play, just be normal, without the worry that someone might mention something that makes you feel abnormal, like a dead parent. Everyone at the Dougy Center has a dead parent. That is the norm. Anything that helped India feel connected to her peers was a miracle.

While the kids played, the parents got to sit in a room with each other and talk, or not talk, as well. We usually talked about solo parenting. We could commiserate with each other because, for each of us, it had been a year, or years, since we had gone to the bathroom alone. That's a grief thing that no one thinks about. India wouldn't leave my side, not even for a bathroom break, lest I die too. At the Dougy Center, I realized that it was not just my child; it was everyone's child. We congratulated each other when our kids made it to school on time and empathized when they didn't. I was able to talk about being mad at Dan for leaving me here alone, and no one judged me. We were allowed to laugh at the idiocy of grief without people thinking we should be crying instead. At the Dougy Center, dead spouses, and dead parents, were the norm. India and I needed to feel normal again, if only for an hour. The Dougy Center is an amazing place and is nationally recognized for its work with grieving children. Many cities have programs that emulate them. If you are grieving, please find a support group.

For more than a year I drove back and forth to therapy and support group while India raged. I just kept driving. The second year, she begrudgingly got in the car and complained, but didn't rage. Eventually she resigned herself to going. After three years she now gets in the car happily, and we've made it there and back in a good mood. This winter we missed support group because of a snow day, and when she looked on the calendar and saw it was Dougy night, she was actually disappointed that we couldn't go. It took three years to get to that point.

India could not express her emotions about Dan. The few times India talked about Dan, it was in very short little snippets: one sentence, maybe two, and then she would change the subject. Those moments were, and are, precious to me.

"Mommy, I'm gonna say a funny Daddy word. Are you ready? Nincompoop. Isn't that a funny Daddy word?" Dan used to say that word all the time.

One day, she spilled 7UP all down her arm, laughed about it, and said, "I'll bet if Daddy were here, he would be laughing at me right now."

I told her once, "Baby Girl, your Daddy was really silly."

"I know, Mommy. That's what made him Daddy."

At bedtime one night I asked, "India, where do you want to go for dreamland tonight?"

"I don't know."

"Well, where do you think Daddy would want to go?"

She thought for a long moment. "Home," she said.

A note from Dan:

> *I would write a poem about how grateful I am that you are India's Mommy. I would write how safe and secure that makes me feel and how proud I am of how you are raising her and how I tell people all the time about the cute things you two do and how I see you in her every day. I would write how hard I know you work and how I know you are always trying to be a good Mommy and even though you sometimes feel like you aren't you really are because otherwise you wouldn't feel that way. I would write and tell you how well prepared for life our daughter is going to be and how that's thanks to you. And I would write how you are an amazing wife and how I am so lucky to be with you.*
>
> *All my love, all my life, forever,*
> *Dan*

I'm trying, Dan. I'm trying.

A year after Dan died, India and I had what I thought was a very good talk about Dan at bedtime. At that point it was nearly the only talk we've ever had about him. It started with her goofing around and not settling down for bed.

I said, "Oh, if Daddy were here, he would be tickling you so bad right now," which made her laugh. Then I said, "Well, where is Daddy?" By this time she had settled down and was lying on her back with her arms stretched up in the air.

"I don't know where he is," she said. I laid on my back and stretched my arms up in the air.

"Daddy is in heaven," I said. "He lives there now. Let's pretend that our arms can stretch all the way to heaven and reach Daddy. What would they do? Mine would give him a big hug. A giant hug."

She grabbed my arm with her hands and pulled it down to her. She hung on to me as tightly as she could.

"That's what mine would do," she said. I asked her why she never talked about Daddy.

"I don't know," she answered.

"Do you think it will make Mommy too sad? Because it's okay if it does."

"No."

"Do you think it will make YOU too sad?" She didn't answer. I told her that it was okay to be sad about Daddy, and that it was okay to be mad about Daddy, and that it was okay to talk about Daddy and be sad. Then I told her that I liked talking about Daddy, because it makes me feel better. She didn't have a response, but she heard me.

Two years after Dan died, I had a parent meeting with MTD. We do that every six weeks or so to discuss how India is doing and what is going on. I tell him I suck at parenting and he tells me I'm doing a great job. We talk about Dan. I ask for advice on how to help my child.

At this particular meeting, he very gently told me he thought India was depressed and anxious, and would like to refer us to a child psychiatrist to be evaluated for medication. He looked concerned as I started to cry.

"What are you thinking?" he asked.

I answered, "Honestly, I'm not surprised. I've been wondering the same thing for a while now. It just sucks."

Two years of pretending and acting like she was fine had caught up to her. She was not fine. She was trying to control life, when life was completely out of her control. MTD described how depression is displayed in children.

Anxious? Check. Afraid to do things? Check. Easily irritated? Double check. Easily angered? Definitely check. Plus, she had stopped wanting to play with her friends. She never wanted to go do anything, except stay home and watch television. She was not my happy, on-top-of-the-world, little girl. I didn't expect her to be. Dan died, of course she was not the same. No one could be. But this wasn't what I wanted for her either.

I felt like I had failed her. I couldn't talk to her, I couldn't get her to understand. I couldn't get her to talk about her Daddy. She had closed herself off, and I couldn't help her, no matter how much I tried. We were at an impasse. She seemed to get worse by the day: more anxious, more angry, more sad.

MTD and I explained to India that she needed to see "The Special Dr. Martha."

"Because we know you don't feel good. You're home sick from school a lot, your tummy always hurts, everything is scary, you get upset all the time. We're going to see this doctor, and she will help you feel better." How do you tell a nine-year-old girl that she's depressed? Does she even know what that means, depression? Does she understand? All India knew is that her tummy hurt, every single time we left the house.

We went to the specialist, Martha. She agreed with MTD and prescribed antidepressants for my Baby Girl. My Baby Girl was no longer fearless. I used to say she could conquer the world, but now I wondered if we would make it through fourth grade. The thought of high school was terrifying. India went to the special doctor without a fight. India took her pill without a fight. India knew that something was not right, and she needed help with feeling safe and secure and in control of just a little bit of her own life.

A lot of other parents judged me for "drugging" my child. I didn't care. She needed help, and I was willing to do whatever it took to help her.

It took a month for the medication to start working. We went to see Dr. Martha for a checkup, and she asked me if I noticed anything yet. I thought maybe so. She was talking more. Not about her dad, of course, but more chatter. She used to talk non-stop, and then she stopped. I didn't really notice until it started to come back. She was more engaged. She didn't seem to be in her own little world as much. It was definitely doing something. Her anxiety was sky high, and had been, since the day her dad died. It was not helping with her depression. The doctor raised the dosage.

A month later, we went back for another checkup, and Dr. Martha asked me if I thought it was helping yet. At that point, there was no longer any doubt.

India had gone to a slumber party with her friends. She hadn't done that in I don't know how long. I had explained to the mom in charge that India's anxiety worsened at night, and asked her to call me if India wanted to come home. Nobody called. I picked her up the next day and she had had a great time. She had told one of her friends that she went to therapy. That was huge. I know it sounds ridiculous, but it was huge. She had never told any of her friends about therapy before. She had gone to great lengths to be normal, and therapy was not normal.

Before meds, I had to walk her into her class every morning and let her get all settled before she reluctantly said goodbye. The week before our checkup with Dr. Martha, she said goodbye in the hall and even let me drop her off at the curb, twice. That was huge.

I had parent-teacher conferences and her teacher told me how great she was doing. "She's active and engaged and happy! It's like she's a whole new kid!" No, she's not a whole new kid. What her teacher was seeing was a glimpse of the kid I used to have, before her Daddy died. I'm sorry you didn't know her then. I'm sorry that all you've known is the sad, frightened kid that was left, because my kid is amazing. My kid can conquer the world, if we can get her out the front door.

Antidepressants work. They don't cure death. They don't work every day. Sometimes it is still just too much for her little heart and brain to deal with.

One day they did not work. I had an extremely busy week, and she didn't see a lot of me, which I know is a recipe for anxiety. All morning India said that she didn't feel good, that she wanted to stay home, and that her tummy hurt. We had an appointment with MTD and then another one with Dr. Martha. She flat out refused to talk to MTD. She didn't say a single word and tried to leave several times.

MTD called Dr. Martha before we got there, to warn her that India was having a really bad day. India also refused to talk to Dr. Martha, but it was clear that she was very unhappy and angry. She kept punching her fists into her seat and being aggressive with the toys. The doctor is wise, and it was a short appointment.

As we left the office and walked down the hall, India slumped against the wall, slid to the floor, and cried. Crying in public is not something India does.

"I don't want to be here. I want to be home," she wailed. I get it. When I say something like that, it's code for "life is too hard today and I want to be snuggled in a blanket watching TV next to Dan." I don't want to go to therapy. I don't want to deal with grief. I don't want to be sad, but I can't make myself happy right now. Antidepressants help. But there is no cure for a dead Daddy.

Right now, she has been on the antidepressants for a little over a year. At our last appointment with Dr. Martha, we decided it was time to lower the dosage. We haven't seen any effects of that yet. It's too soon. Life is slowly getting better for her. She is slowly getting the hang of releasing her emotions in healthy ways. She is slowly becoming okay with talking about Daddy. She is slowly starting to admit that she misses him.

India had a dream about Dan. This is also unusual, or at least, it's unusual for her to tell me about it. She woke up all smiles and happiness one day, and said, "Mommy! I just had the best dream ever! Me and you and Daddy and Auntie Pauline were all at the Mall of America, and we were riding all the rides. Then just Daddy and I went on the obstacle course and it was really cool. Then just Daddy and I went on the zip line and it was really fun." They never did this exact thing, but it's the exact thing they would have done together.

That's what she did with her Daddy. They went on wild adventures, they climbed rocks, they slid down hills. She remembers that. He was her adventure buddy. I used to picture the trouble they would get into when she was a little older: upside down roller coasters, bungee jumping, skydiving. They would have done it all. Instead, it's just a dream, even if it was a really good dream.

At another parent meeting with MTD, he told me in the nicest, kindest way possible that I was "pushing" grief on India, and she couldn't go on with life that way. I had to give her space to just be. I knew he was right, and I didn't want him to be. I wasn't trying to push grief on her; I just didn't want her to forget her Daddy. Here is

195

what MTD meant: I wanted her to talk about him. I constantly brought up the subject of Dan. He was in every conversation. I worked him in. I knew I did that, because to me he should be a part of every conversation. He should BE here for the conversation. For India, he didn't need to be in every conversation, because he's not a part of every conversation.

"But I don't want her to forget him," I told MTD through tears. Truly, it's my biggest fear.

"She won't, I promise," he said. "She will remember him better if she's not being forced to, if you just let it come naturally. Some things she will remember years later or even when she is a grown up. She can't remember them now. It's too much for her little brain and her little heart. She has to push them aside so she can get through every day, and that's okay. That's what kids do."

"I understand what you're saying, but I can't just not talk about Dan, I can't," I told him.

"I'm not telling you to stop talking about Dan. Just let it come more naturally, don't force it."

I will try it, but it will be HARD. Every single night, I tell her I love her, and I add, "and Daddy loves you, too." I have to say it for him, because he's not here to say it himself. That's how I feel. But it's not how India feels. She knows Dan loves her, and she doesn't need me to tell her every night. She doesn't need me to say the things Daddy would have said. She doesn't want me to, either. Those sayings were Daddy's. Not mine.

I can't let Dan go. I can't make room for anything else right now. My whole life was with him. India has a whole life ahead of her. She needs to have the room to fill it up with joy, and not sadness. She wants to have room for Dan and her whole big life. I was not letting her do that, even though that's exactly what I want for her. It was one of those things I didn't realize I'd been doing, until someone pointed it out to me. I was constantly reminding her about her dad, because I am constantly reminded of her dad and I say it out loud.

"You roll your eyes just like your Daddy."

"You have the same eyes as Daddy."

"You like to collect things like Daddy."

"You sound just like Daddy."

"We used to go to that store with Daddy."

"We used to go to that park with Daddy. Do you remember?"

When you put it all together like that, it does sound pushy, although it was unintentional. I think about Dan all the time. So, I mentioned Dan all the time. But after a long talk with her therapist, I decided to make a concentrated effort to not "push" Dan on India. I would not ask her if she remembered doing such and such with Daddy. I would not ask her if she missed Daddy. I would give her space to be.

Did I mention my daughter is contrary? I'm pretty sure she gets it from her dad. I talked about Dan less, so she started talking about Dan more. Out of nowhere, she would mention something about Dan. She talked about things they used to do together. She told her auntie all about the half-written story she found of his, and how she is going to finish it for him and show it to the world. That was huge. Auntie Melinda gave India an old backpack of Dan's. I had given it to her after Dan died. India found it at Melinda's house and thought it was cool.

She took that backpack with us everywhere we went for three days. She told anyone that would listen all about how it used to be Daddy's. "It was Daddy's, and now I get it."

I told my therapist this story and she said, "It almost sounds like India is proud of it. Proud that is was Dan's."

"She is," I said.

"India is proud of her Daddy, perhaps not sad like you, but proud," my therapist mused.

In one month after starting the whole "no pushing" plan, India talked more about her dad than she did in the previous two years. Dan was a therapist. He always thought he was right, too.

She has started asking questions about him. I wish with every cell in my body that I didn't have to answer for her. I wish she could just remember how he hated coffee, and a Bismarck was his favorite donut. Mountain Dew was his favorite soda. He hated mint and wouldn't even kiss me if I had eaten anything with mint. He loved eggs. I just told her today that before she was born, he had knee surgery. If Dan had lived, that knee surgery would have been updated this last year and she would have known all about it.

India woke up another morning and said, "Mommy I had the best dream ever." Usually when she tells me this, it is about her stuffed animals, or being a princess, or some other typical kid dream. So, I said, "Oh, I can't wait to hear about it. Tell me!" She told me a dream I was not expecting.

"I was playing at the neighbor's house and you were walking across the street to come get me. I looked out of their window and Daddy was walking beside you coming to get me, too. I ran out the front door and ran to Daddy as fast as I could. I ran and ran. Then Daddy scooped me up and I gave him kisses and hugs and snuggles; lots and lots and lots and he never put me down."

It's possibly the best dream I've ever heard. It was the best dream ever. Daddy was alive, and right here in our house, and giving her hugs and kisses. Why can't this be real? Why does my kid have to have dreams about her Daddy? Why can't she have the real thing?

One night we were driving home from the Dougy Center. As I was driving, she said, "Mommy it's not fair!"

"What's not fair?"

"We always go around the circle and say how our person died, and then we get to say our favorite movie or color, and I always have to say 'pass' because I don't know how Daddy died. So I never get to tell anyone my favorite thing, and that's not fair." Play it cool, Jenny. Play it cool.

"I can tell you how Daddy died. Would you like me to?"

"Okay, I guess."

"Daddy died of a seizure. So, when people ask you, just say he had a seizure and died."

"I don't know what a seizure is, but okay."

"I can tell you what a seizure is. Would you like me to tell you?"

"Nope," she said, and instantly changed the subject. At that time, it had been 21 months since Dan died, and she didn't know. She said pass at every single grief group because she didn't have the right answer. I know I didn't flat out tell her he had died of a seizure. She has never ever asked me a single thing about him dying. I didn't tell her because she didn't ask. At the same time, I didn't hide it from her either. I would talk about it with other grownups in her presence; it wasn't a secret. I guess I just assumed or rather wanted to assume that she picked up on it when she overheard me talking.

At the beginning of her fifth-grade school year in 2017, I told India's new teacher our story. You know, the one about how in the middle of second grade I woke India up in the middle of the night to tell her that her Daddy was dead. That's always a great story to start the year off with. I figure it's better to get it over with. Maybe it will create less awkwardness later. I told her about how hard life has been since then and how this grief thing is worse than most people can possibly imagine. I told her about how India (and I) had basically been shut down for the last two years.

She responded with, "Well, how could you not?" It was then that I knew this teacher got us. This teacher had our backs. We had had a really good summer. I finally felt like maybe we could deal with this grief thing. I relayed this information to her teacher and how I wanted to keep this good momentum going.

At parent teacher conferences that October, India got glowing reviews, and one small criticism. She tended to be a bit of a chatterbox. I looked at my child and she gave me a sly little smile. I said, "Oh really?" to her teacher, but in my brain, I was doing that thing where you raise your fist in the air and bring your elbow down as you're screaming, "YES!!!" This is my child. This is my child who started talking at nine months. This is my child, who was speaking in full sentences by her first birthday. This is my child, who in preschool had over half the class mesmerized as she told them stories at recess. This is my child, who I used to wish would just stop talking for five seconds while we were in the car. When her Daddy died her world became sadly, eerily silent. She stopped talking in the car. This is when her principal said she never talked in school. This is when it seemed like only one person, her favorite teacher, could get her to say anything at all. This is when she stopped telling stories. It just stopped. All her talking stopped. She barely even talked to me. Perhaps it's because her all-time favorite person to talk to was dead, and the rest of us simply wouldn't do.

After that conference I had a parent meeting with MTD. I told him about how at conferences her teacher had said she was a bit of a chatterbox. He didn't have to do it in his head. He punched his fist up in the air, brought his elbow down, and yelled "YES!" He knows India pretty well by now; he knows this is a huge step for her.

Her Daddy would be so proud of her. I can imagine him punching his fist in the air and bringing his elbow down and saying, "YES! THAT'S MY GIRL!" I just wish I could really see him do it instead of imagining it.

It's been three years of therapy and grief support group, and one year of being on antidepressants. Is it working? It depends on what we are trying to do, exactly. Take her pain away? Take her grief away? Impossible. That is not the goal. We want her to be able to live, despite the grief, beside the grief. We want her to have a great life; we want her to be happy. I am certain that's what Dan would want for her too. So, is that working?

It's helping. It is getting so much better. She no longer has grief tantrums every day, or even every week. It's been more than a month since her last one. She is slowly becoming a part of the world again. She is more open. She has much less anxiety. She doesn't look scared all the time anymore, and sometimes I can even see the sparkle come back into her eye.

MTD said something interesting. It never occurred to me before, but he said that over the past three years, she has been processing all this grief internally. She is an internal thinker. That's when I realized that of course she is. She is exactly like her father. Dan was always an internal processor. It used to drive me nuts, and India is exactly like Dan. Then MTD said something even more amazing. He said she has done so much grief work that he is astounded. He would estimate she has done five years' worth of normal child's grief work in three years. I guess we have come a long way. That's my kid, the internal overachiever. She's exactly like her father. Maybe she can conquer the world after all.

CHAPTER 15:

It's Quiet Uptown

∞ ∞ ∞

As one grows, certain things inevitably change. The way we look at the world, the way we look at other people, and the way we look at ourselves all changes as time passes. If we're lucky, some things will stay the same. Hopefully, our mother will always in some ways be "Mommy" and our father will be the "great advice giver". If we are truly, truly lucky, then the house we grew up in will always be home.
— Dan Stults

Hey, you know what's a shitty thing to do? To send a text to your mother-in-law when she is four states away, fifteen months after her son dies, while everyone is still reeling and wondering what catastrophe will happen next, that says, "Do you want the bad news now or when you get home?" Don't do that to her. Preface it with "NOBODY DIED" and then tell her. Always preface bad news that way, unless someone did die, and then you are screwed. Yet that's exactly what I did one Friday evening in April 2016.

My entire life had just been ripped out from under me, AGAIN. I hadn't even gotten it together from it being ripped apart the first time. I was still in shock. I was still in utter survival mode. I was barely functioning. And now this. Pat didn't text me back. Instead, she called me within seconds.

"What is it?" she cried. I couldn't bear to say it. I started crying hysterically.

"Jennifer, tell me what's going on!"

Could she even understand what I said through my hysterics? "My house! They are selling my house. I have to get out."

I have often heard that when people lose their spouse, they lose their homes, income, and friends, too. I can attest to that. It's so much more than just losing your true love. As if that wasn't bad enough, but you also lose your entire way of life, down to the place you call home.

Our first home together was an apartment. It was the first place we lived as man and wife. Newlywed bliss seeped through the walls of that home. The sun shone through the windows so brightly. Hope was everywhere. Young love, so cute it was sickening. We made that tiny space a beautiful home. We were barely old enough to be married. Our whole lives were just beginning in that home. Love bloomed in that home.

Then, our home was a run-down trailer in a run-down trailer park. That home was a pit. We hated living there, but we loved being together. We turned the pit into a home. We spent lots of time studying in that home, writing papers, preparing for our careers. The walls were so thin the heat never stayed in. It was okay, though. It meant more cuddling together. Love survived in that home.

We moved out of that pit and into a real apartment. It felt huge in comparison. Great times with friends abounded in that home. We laughed and laughed at each other in that home. We both graduated from college in that home. Love flourished in that home.

Our next home was a transitional home: a room in the garage at Dan's parents' house. Dan's old room. We had just moved back to Oregon from college in Idaho and hadn't found a place to live yet. It was small, but it was home, and we made it ours. We spent lots of time with family in that home. Love was old and familiar in that home.

After that we lived in a small cottage on church land. We worked hard in that home. We saved and saved in that home. We went on the trip of a lifetime while living in that home. We found out I was pregnant in that home. Love was content in that home.

We bought our first house. Two stories, a house home, in the city. It was either yellow or cream depending on if you asked me or Dan, we both agreed that the trim was dark green. That home was full of misadventures. Leaky faucets and flooded basements. Love grew from two to three in that home. Baby Girl was born in that home. She learned to walk and talk in that home. Love had us wrapped around her little finger in that home.

Four years ago, our home was brown with red trim. Daddy, Mommy, India. It was full of giggles and laughter and unimaginable goofiness. We played in treehouses and on rope swings. We had hopes of growing more love in that home. Love had so much fun in that home.

Three years ago, it was the same house, but the home had changed. The home was now full of unimaginable sorrow. India and I screamed and raged in pain. It hurt in that home. The sorrow tried to drag us down, and we might have allowed it to, if not for the love. Love was there, alongside the sorrow, in that home.

> *Sometimes the most adult thing you can do is ask for help when you need it.*
> — *Buffy the Vampire Slayer*

Fifteen months after Dan died, I was just starting to get my feet under me. I felt like maybe, just maybe, we could make it. I hoped. I had recently been to Dr. Ava for anxiety pills and antidepressants and that was helping a lot. One day, as I was grocery shopping with my cousin, my phone rang. I answered my phone as she ran off to the bathroom. It was my landlord.

"I have some news. The owner wants to sell the house."

"I'll buy it!" I said. I had no intention of moving out, ever. This was the last house we lived in with Dan. "I'll buy it right now. How much does he want?" She told me. It turns out that everyone wants to move to Oregon, and housing prices in my area were skyrocketing. I didn't fall on the floor right there, but only because I was holding on to a shopping cart. There was no way I could afford my own house. I didn't have that much money and I knew I couldn't get a loan for that much money. There was, flat out, no way.

"What other options do I have?" I asked.

"You have 90 days to move out," she replied. I had just lost my husband and now, without any choice or any control, I was losing my house. How could this be happening? People who don't pay their rent get kicked out. We always paid our rent right on time. People who are loud and obnoxious get kicked out; we were quiet and well behaved. It made no sense. AGAIN, the world was making no sense. These things just don't happen. Husbands don't die of seizures and people don't get kicked out of their houses for no reason. This isn't how life works. This isn't my life; this isn't what happens to me.

By the time my cousin came back from the bathroom, I was crying hysterically, and two strangers were holding me up and trying to ask me what happened. I couldn't even get the words out of my mouth. My cousin came up to me and I collapsed into her arms and cried. She had no idea what was going on. I was fine two minutes ago. I think she thought I was having a grief attack. We left our carts in the middle of the store and left without me explaining anything. In the car, I was able to tell her what happened. She was shocked and had some choice words for my landlord.

That evening after I dropped India off at a slumber party, I sent the text to my mother-in-law and she called me. I don't remember exactly what she said, but she knew how much our home meant to me. She cried along with me. Then she said something that was utterly astonishing and yet so exactly like her that I think I knew all along she would say it.

"Move in with us. We will take care of you."

"OK."

The one catch to living with Dan's parents was that their house was not within the boundaries of India's school district. India would have to change schools. NO, NO, NO. HARD NO. I was not playing that game. I was not going to do that to her. I could not do that to her. Her school was amazing and supportive when Dan died, and I knew we could find a way to work this out. I was not going to make her change schools, too. I just wasn't.

After a PTA meeting, I asked the principal if I could talk to him for a minute. He could tell immediately that something was up.

"You look like you are in a transition. Did you get a job?" Oh man, I wish I had gotten a job that would have been so much easier. No, I did not get a job. I got kicked out of my house instead. I explained the situation to him: that we would be moving in with my in-laws until I could find a house in the school district, which I was determined to do.

"Please, please, please don't make India switch schools. She needs to stay where she feels safe. I can drive her back and forth, please," I begged.

He looked at me incredulously and said simply, "India's not going anywhere; we are not doing that to her. She belongs here. We will figure something out." I was surprised and relieved to hear him say that, but I knew all along that's what he was going to say.

In our school district, anything that is not living in your own home qualifies you as homeless. Moving into the loving, warm home of your grandparents counts as homelessness. Homelessness has few perks, but there is one benefit to being classified in this way: homeless children cannot be forced to leave their school, and India got to stay, no matter what. All I had to do was sign a paper saying we were homeless. It was not exactly where I thought my life would be, and definitely not where it was headed.

Now, I had to tell India we were moving. I can't describe the giant pit in my stomach just thinking about telling her. I called MTD, hoping he would have some advice on how to destroy her life yet again, as nicely as possible. The basic consensus was to rip the Band-Aid off. Get it over with as soon as possible, so I would have time to pack and she has time to grieve this loss as well. It took me a few days to build up the courage to do it. When she came home from school that day, I told her I wanted her to come rockabye with me because I needed to tell her something. We always had big conversations while we rockabyed.

I don't remember my exact words, but I remember her reaction. She screamed in anguish. Tears streamed down her face. From the outside, it probably looked as if she was more upset about moving than she was when I told her that Daddy had died. I think the difference was that she knew what moving meant. We have moved before, and she could grasp the concept of moving. She couldn't grasp the concept of Dan's death. She started to rage.

"I AM NOT MOVING! THEY CAN'T MAKE ME! THIS IS MY HOUSE!" I had no argument. There was nothing I could say; I felt exactly the same way, except I knew they could make us. I cried with her. The next day, through my tears, I started packing.

I had to pack up all of our things, all of his things. I had to decide which of Dan's things I was going to keep. There would be no going through it slowly and casually, like I had intended. I was not ready to do it, but once again, I had no choice in the matter. I packed Dan's keys. They had been hanging on the key hook ever since he died. I hadn't touched them. Now they were in a box, and I wouldn't take them out again, because it's not like he's going to use them. He's not coming back. He didn't need his keys. I wasn't quite expecting that one little thing to hurt my heart as badly as it did, but I suppose my subconscious knew, because I had left them up there. The next time I came home and hung my keys on the hook, his weren't there. That was hard to swallow.

I also got rid of some big sentimental things, because I didn't think they would move well. The leftover dried flowers from the funeral. A jar full of dried flowers in oil that were parts of all the flowers Dan had given me while we were dating. The dried roses Dan gave me the day I went into labor with India. We didn't know I'd be going into labor. I was just so sick of being pregnant and he was trying to make me feel better, so he got me roses. My water broke twenty minutes later.

I took all of these things into our backyard and burned them in our fire pit. I also burned Dan's hoard of papers. Recycling them didn't feel right. Throwing the flowers in the trash didn't feel right. Burning them felt right. They no longer existed. Like our marriage. Like Dan.

I let go of so many of Dan's things. Some things WERE Dan and I got rid of them anyway. I just couldn't keep it all. Some things, though, I couldn't get rid of. Dan loved collecting rocks. Every time we left the house he came back with a rock, or two, or a bucket full. The really nice ones were on display in the house, the semi nice ones were on display in the garage. The plain ones were contained in a giant flower bed in the front yard. As I was packing up our lives, someone asked me about the rocks.

"Leave them," they said. "It's way too much work for you to pack them all up." I shrugged and continued packing other things. Then one day, I packed the rocks. They were Dan's rocks and I couldn't leave them behind. I pulled them ALL out of the yard and laid them out in my garage so they could dry out and be packed. Every single one. They had been pushed into the dirt over the years and were wet and covered in leaves and pine needles. Still, I dug them all out. Several people told me it was not necessary, that I didn't need to do all that work. I didn't need all those, just a few would do. I packed them anyway. The neighbor lady asked what I was doing, and I told her.

"Crazy, huh?" I said.

"Doesn't sound crazy at all to me," she replied.

On moving day, friends came over and helped us put boxes into a pod. Boxes and boxes and boxes of rocks. Some of the rocks were too big for a box.

Several people commented, "Wow! You have a lot of rocks. Why are you keeping all these rocks? What are you going to do with all of them?"

I just shrugged and said, "They're Dan's rocks. I can't leave them."

I was a little bitter that we were getting kicked out of our house for no good reason. I felt it was bad enough that they were making me move; I wasn't going to do any deep cleaning or painting. My family and friends were in agreement and we thought of all kinds of crazy ideas to scare away potential buyers. My sisters wanted to stand in the front yard and tell everyone who came to look at the house that Dan had died in it. We thought about setting up pulleys and flashing lights, so the house appeared haunted. Some friends offered to picket the open houses with signs that said "He's kicking out a young widow", "You're traumatizing a child", and "He died on the living room floor". The best idea we came up with was to draw an outline of Dan's body on the living room floor with Sharpie. Exactly as he laid. I can tell you, I remember. We all loved this idea. It's exactly what Dan would have done. In the end, of course, we didn't do anything. We just moved.

I'm the only person I knew that actually enjoyed moving. I liked packing things, organizing things. I'm good at it and I enjoy it. Not this time. I couldn't do it; my mind wasn't there. I could barely pack. I had many, many days where friends would come over and help me pack. They would just put my stuff in boxes for me, because I literally couldn't do it. I couldn't concentrate on it, couldn't focus, couldn't believe this was happening. It was more trauma, and I couldn't handle more trauma.

Moving day came. Our entire life together was going to three different places: clothes and stuff we use daily went to my in-laws' house; outside things, like the swing set and the trampoline, went to my dad's house for storage; everything else went into a moving pod. Lots of people were coming over to help, probably more people than have ever gone to a moving party. I didn't want to be there; I didn't want to do this. India didn't either, but she had become very good at pushing her emotions aside by now, so she just ignored the whole thing and played with her friends.

I was trying to prepare myself. "Okay, Jenny. Take deep breaths. I can do this. This is happening."

Mari showed up first. She had a six-month-old baby. Before I could even say hello, she strapped the baby sling to me and put her baby in it.

"Your only job today is to hold this baby. We've got everything else," she said. That's what I did. I held Mari's beautiful baby all day long, and everyone moved my house for me. I didn't lift a single box.

I was slightly hesitant to move in with Dan's parents. I didn't want to burden them or be in the way. I was worried about India leaving her toys all over the floor and Grandpa tripping over them and falling. I was worried about India having grief tantrums at their house and how they would handle it. I was worried that I would love being taken care of and never want to leave. If I let them take care of me, what motivation do I have to take care of myself? Won't I just get more depressed with nothing to worry about? And what motivation would there be for me to ever move out? I was afraid I would say it was for six months, and I'd be there for three years with no reason to leave.

I voiced my concerns to Jill, and she came back with this, "It might be really good for you to have some time where you are not responsible for a lot of the day-to-day care of a household. You can focus on yourself and India. Eventually, you'll have to get back to the household care, but if you have a chance to focus your energy somewhere else, take it. India is having a hard time being around Grandma and Grandpa because they are different, because they are sad. This might be an opportunity for all of you to heal a little bit together."

The weekend after school was out, we moved in with my in-laws. Not because I had no place else to go, but because this was the best place for us to go. They would take care of us, they loved us, they are our family.

We went back to our safe home, to Dan's parent's home. That home was full of sorrow, too. But beside that sorrow was also love. We rested in that home, we found some strength in that home. Love enveloped us in that home.

I remember Pat telling me, "The only thing I want you to do here is rest. You need to rest." That's basically all I did; she wouldn't let me do anything else. I didn't cook or clean. I didn't even do laundry. I rested. I took a nap almost every day, and I watched a lot of mindless TV. I spent time playing with India, and held her when she had grief tantrums. I looked for a house for us to live in. I contemplated just living with them forever, letting them take care of us forever.

While we were living with my in-laws, I was invited to a weekend women's retreat. The theme for the weekend was HOME. The first thing we had to do was make name tags that told about our home. Really? I thought. She's gonna make me do this? And now it's decision time. Do you make something flowery and pretty or do you tell the truth?

I decided to do both. I used my favorite color paper I used glitter, and then I taped and cut and taped and cut until it looked like it was broken and being put back together. That was a pretty good description of my "home". Then I put a broken black ribbon on it for Dan. I didn't do a very good job with the glue, and it fell apart. That seemed fitting. The first thing we did was sit in tables and describe our name tags.

"Hi. I'm Jenny. My name tag represents being broken and torn because that's what home feels like right now." The three people at the table who knew me nodded their heads in understanding. The three that didn't wondered what the heck I was talking about.

The next question was "where is home?" I could be practical, and tell everyone what city I lived in, but clearly, she was looking for a more metaphorical answer. We go around the table and everyone says things like:

"My family is my home."

"My church makes me feel at home."

"Wherever my husband and I are together is home."

Now it's my turn, and it's decision time again. Lollipops and rainbows, or the truth?

"My home is a little broken at the moment. My husband died last year, so that part of my home is gone. And then we had to move out of our physical home, so that part of home is gone, too." Tears fill my eyes. I don't mention that India and I aren't the same as we used to be, so we don't feel like home either. Not the home we used to have.

Next question. "Where do you feel at home?" Since we ended with me, we started with me. Nowhere. I used to feel at home with Dan. It didn't matter where we were. He was my home. I imagine putting my head on his chest. I can feel his warmth, feel his breathing, feel his heartbeat, feel his arms around me. Now I'm really crying.

"Ever since he died, I haven't felt at home. I've just felt lost. I'm lost without him. I don't think I will feel at home until I'm with him again in heaven, and that is so long from now!" I put my head down on the table and try to control my tears. Someone pats my back and the person next to me takes their turn answering the question. I can't do it. I can't stop crying. I can't be here. I get up and leave, looking for somewhere to hide.

I go into the sanctuary. All the lights are off and it's totally dark, a great hiding place. I lie down in one of the pews and sob. Damn it, Dan. Why did you die? I need you, I miss you. I lie there and cry for Dan. I look up at the stained-glass window. I'm crying for my dead husband and I'm angry at God. Dan's death has wrecked another place where I used to feel at home. I don't anymore. I grew up Catholic. As soon as I would walk into a sanctuary, peace would come over me, a feeling of home. I haven't felt that in a sanctuary since Dan died.

My friend comes to find me, and we talk for a while. She tells me how I'm so strong, and a great mom, and I'm making it through this so well. I want to laugh because I don't feel like any of those things, but I know she loves me and I know she's sincere. We wait until almost everyone else leaves for the night, and then we go get my things to go home.

I had to find somewhere for India and me to live, permanently. We needed somewhere we could try to be happy. I had two requirements: First, I was going to buy, not rent, so that no one could ever kick us out again. It would be ours forever. Second, it had to be in the same school district. India would not be changing schools.

This caused two problems: First, I had no job, no spouse with a job, and bad credit. Nobody in their right mind was going to give me a loan. Second, everything in our school district was too expensive. I couldn't afford anything in our area, or I would have stayed in our old home. I was pretty sure I was screwed.

Through a friend, I got in touch with a realtor who was an expert in our area. I told her what I was looking for and what my budget was, and she said, "I'm sorry; that doesn't exist. You can't do it." I told her I didn't have a choice; that this is what I needed to do. I told her my "sob story" about my dead husband and getting kicked out of my house.

"I am going to find you a house, don't you worry. I will find you a house," she said.

She hooked me up with a mortgage broker who said I couldn't get a loan with my bad credit. I told her my "sob story", and she said, "I will get you a loan. We will make this work," and they did. They both worked magic.

We started house hunting. It wasn't going well. Everything was in the wrong location or cost too much, but there was one house. I looked at pictures online and was not interested. My realtor convinced me to go look at it anyway. I did. The location was perfect. However, it was the ugliest house I had ever laid eyes on and I did not want to live there. We kept looking, with no luck.

"Let's look at that one again," she suggested. We did. It was still the ugliest house I'd ever seen and had a ton of things wrong with it: it needed a new roof, the septic tank was bad, the plumbing didn't work, and it had a rotten deck. Did I mention that it was ugly?

"You can fix all that!" my realtor said. She was right, of course. I just didn't want to do all that work. I was still so tired all the time. "It's the only thing you can afford in this area," she continued. "And look! It's a sign!" It was literally a street sign. This house was on the corner of Dan's Avenue. I told her I didn't believe in signs and proceeded to buy the ugliest house in existence.

It is a mile away from our old house. It's almost exactly the same as our old house, right down to layout and square footage. It's in a great neighborhood. Kids for India to play with abound. The neighbors are so nice and have taken on the job of watching out for the young widow and her daughter. It's a great little house. It's ugly as all get out, but it is a great little house.

It took longer to fix up the house than I anticipated. We continued to live with Pat and Al while we did so. I suppose, like all houses, it was just one thing after another that needed to be fixed. I did as much work as I could by myself. My friends helped. My brother-in-law, who is a handy man, did most of it and what he couldn't do I hired people to do. Most of them gave me good deals after hearing my story and saying, "But you're way too young to be a widow!" I agree. It showed me yet again that there are good people in the world. I had a new roof put on and a new septic tank put in. We had all new windows and new doors put in. We gutted the bathroom and repiped everything. I splurged on an extra deep soaking tub. I told everyone, "If I have to do this widow thing and buy a house all by myself, I am going to have a damn nice bathtub."

Since I am not a skilled handy person, I did grunt work like ripping out the carpet, sanding, and varnishing the floors. I tore down the rotten deck, ripped apart the broken hot tub, and knocked out a closet wall. Two rooms were covered in hideous wood paneling from the 1970's. My sister and I ripped it all down, only to find another layer of wood paneling behind it. So, we ripped that down, too. I had a giant pile of stuff in my backyard to be hauled to the dump. When it was gone, I made another huge pile.

I made all the curtains. I wallpapered one room and painted the rest in colors I wanted, except for the bathroom and India's room which were colors that she wanted. I poured my broken soul into fixing this house. I poured my anger at Dan and at God into the energy I needed to fix this house. I guess you could say it was therapeutic.

My friends told me I needed to have a housewarming party. People will bring presents, they said. It will be something happy for you to celebrate, they said. I knew they had a point, but my heart wasn't in it. Grief is like living in two different worlds. In the first one, you know you are lucky, you know you have good things. You love your new little house and are excited to decorate it. You want to have your friends come over and tell you how great it looks. You want to be happy about this "new chapter" in your life. But in the second world, your husband is still dead, and you don't understand how you are breathing without him. That pretty much squashes everything else. Who cares about a party when your love is still dead?

We had a party anyway. I woke up that morning with some pretty big anxiety. Why am I doing this? What's the point? Why am I doing anything? I should just cancel it. We should just stay home and hide under the covers. That sounds way better. We got up and showed up anyway. After all, it was my party. People came, and it was good to see them. They brought presents. I showed them around our tiny little house, too small for tours. I gave tours anyway.

"We still need to fix this and this and this," I said, over and over. "No, we haven't moved in yet; it's not ready."

"This will be really good for you guys," everyone said.

"Yes" I replied, "we are excited." It's not a lie, it's just living in one type of world. The one where you want to be happy and you try to be happy, hoping if you can just act happy for long enough, eventually you will be happy again. The other world was there too. They exist simultaneously, but most people can only see you in one or the other, not both.

In the other world, there is a giant emptiness surrounding you, sucking the energy out of you. The world where you know your husband isn't there with you. The world where everyone seems to be okay with the fact that he's dead, and you're screaming, "It's not okay!" but no one hears you. The world where your sister is trying to be sweet and brings you the flower your husband always brought you, the "symbol" of your love. Then she tells you not to be sad as you stare at it, that she didn't mean to make you sad. Then your friend notices that your introverted husband is not hiding out in a corner somewhere, counting the seconds until everyone goes home, and mentions it to you. You live in both worlds all the time. Everyone else gets to choose which one they live in.

India's anxiety was also huge that day. She was not ready to move into our new house. She wanted to stay at Grandma and Grandpa's where it was safe, and where we were taken care of. Ever since Dan died, large crowds of people overwhelm her. She didn't used to be that way. I wonder if it's because, in the aftermath of Dan's death, so many people were constantly at our house. It's what I needed. I couldn't function without company, but I don't know that it's what India needed. She is her father's daughter, and I know he would have preferred to be alone.

I don't know exactly what happened at the party, if someone said something or if she was simply overwhelmed, but for the first time, she stormed down the hall and into her bedroom. It was empty, but it was her room. She crawled into the closet and shut the closet door. She cried and screamed. I followed her. She had pushed her foot against the closet door so I couldn't open it. I just sat on the floor on the other side of the closet.

"What's the matter, baby?"

"AHHHHHHHHHHHHHHHH!" she wailed, pounding on the wall.

"Honey, can you talk to Mommy?"

"NOOOOOOOOOOOOOO!" I sat outside the closet with tears in my eyes and she sat on the inside doing the same. Why did we do this? Why did I think we could live on our own? I'm not ready to move out. This was all a big mistake. I want to go home, I want Dan. The party goers could hear screaming, and several came to check on us. I shooed them all away. I knew India didn't want them there and didn't want them to see her crying. One bestie, Stacie, refused to leave. She just sat on the ground with me and held my hand as I cried silently because India was crying. Once again, life was too much for my little daughter to handle, and it wasn't fair. I don't remember how, but eventually she calmed down and came out. By then most of the party goers had gone home, back to their homes.

I wanted to bring a picture of Dan over to set on a shelf, but I forgot to grab it. Soon our walls would be covered with pictures of him. We live in both worlds, the one where he is in all our memories and should be with us in our new house, and the one where I painted the walls my favorite color and not his, because he didn't get a vote.

Our new house is about a mile away from our old house, off of a fairly busy street which we drive down regularly. We were driving home one day, and we drove past our old road, which we have done a number of times before.

This time however, India said, "Hey Momma, can we drive past our old house and see if anyone's living in it yet?"

"Sure" I cautiously replied.

It had been almost a year since we were asked to move. We drove down there, and indeed, lights were on and cars were in the driveway. We paused for a minute in front of the house.

Very quietly, in a heartbroken voice, India said, "That's my room...get out. That's my yard...get out. That's my garage...get out. That's my house...get out." Tears rolled down her face. I can't make them get out, Baby Girl. I can't. We drove down the road a little way and turned around to leave.

As we drove back past the house, the sad whisper was gone and a loud angry voice in the back seat yelled, "THAT'S MY ROOM...GET OUT. THAT'S MY YARD... GET OUT. THAT'S MY GARAGE...GET OUT. THAT'S MY HOUSE...GET OUT!" Then she burst into sobs. "I want to go home, I want to go home!" She wasn't talking about the new home a mile away, or our home at Grandma and Grandpa's. She wanted our old home, our old life, her Daddy. There's nothing to say to that. You can't fix that.

I just kept saying, "I know, I know," over and over. It was a long mile. When we got to the house we live in now, India ran inside and slammed the door.

"THIS ISN'T OUR HOUSE! I WANT TO GO HOME." She was pacing around the living room, clenching her fists and crying. She threw herself on the couch and sobbed, "This isn't my house, I want to go home. Mommy, go to our house and tell those other people to get out and they will and then we can go home."

"Oh, how I wish that would work, Baby Girl."

I'm not sure what India pictures when she thinks of that home, but I know what I think of: I picture her, swinging from a rope swing in the middle of summer, and giggling wildly while Dan sprays her with the hose. I picture her "working out" with Dan in the garage. I picture all three of us lying on our bed with our legs up in the air pretending we are riding bicycles upside down. I hear the jingle of Dan's keys every day when he got home from work. I remember the three of us snuggling on the couch watching a movie. That is our home. Dan belongs in our home.

I truly love our new house, and I am so grateful to the people that helped me get it. But it is not the house Dan and I would have picked out together. It is not our dream house, and this is not our dream life. Dan has never seen this new house. Dan did not get to vote on the paint colors. Dan and I will not discuss where the couch should go, or what cupboard to put the dishes in. Dan will not come walking down the hall. Dan will not hog the one bathroom. I swore to Dan that I wouldn't move into another house unless it had two bathrooms, but with one fewer person using it, it wasn't crucial anymore. Dan will not play with India on the living room floor. Dan will not swing her from her rope swing in the backyard. Dan will not bring me coffee as I sit cuddled on the couch on a rainy day. Dan will not hold me at night, and I will not have memories of him in my room. It will be MY room now, not OUR room. We will have no memories of Dan in this house.

I dreamed that he called us. India and I were sitting on the couch at my in-laws' house, the house Dan grew up in. We were watching TV, and India had stolen my phone and was playing a game. My phone rang. I glanced over to see who it was, and it said Dan Stults. India walked away as she answered the phone. "Hi Daddy," she said casually, like it was nothing, something she says every day, like she used to. I could hear him through the phone.

"Hi Baby Girl! Whatcha doing?" I got up and followed her because I wanted to talk to Dan, too. She was pacing back and forth in the bathroom.

"I miss you Daddy! When are you coming home?" I could hear Dan's voice, crystal clear.

"I miss you too, Baby Girl. Don't worry. I'm coming home soon!" I grabbed the phone out of India's hand.

"You're coming home?" I said in amazement. "For real? You're coming home?" Dreams are funny, and even though I was chatting on the phone with my dead husband, I knew perfectly well that he had been dead for two years and two months and two weeks. But he just said he was coming home.

"Yes Jennifer, I'm coming home now. I will see you soon!"

And then I woke up. It was 4:00 AM. I laid in bed, closing my eyes as tightly as I could, trying to go back to sleep so I could finish the dream. So I could get to the part where he came home. So I could get to a part where I could see him and touch him, where I could feel his breath on me as he hugged me. It was a futile effort. You can never get back into a dream once you've gotten out. I laid in bed and tried to replay the dream over and over and over so I wouldn't forget any of it.

It was only a dream. Dan said he was coming home. It was only a dream. Dan said we would see him soon. It was only a dream. It felt so real. It was only a dream. I wish with every atom of my being that it was true. It was only a dream. Dan is still dead. It was only a dream. He's not coming home. It's not possible.

As I type this, we have officially lived in our new house for a year now. I love it, I love it, I love it. I can't describe how much I love it here, I think we can learn to be happy again here. I have tried to incorporate Dan. You can look around and see pieces of him. It makes me feel good. One of India's favorite songs right now is a bluegrass song called "Home". In it is the line, "Home is wherever I'm with you." When I woke her up for school this morning, I sighed and casually said, "I love our home." She hugged me tight and said, "Home is wherever I'm with you."

CHAPTER 16:

I Wrote My Way Out

∞ ∞ ∞

When you feel you can bear it no longer
And that I am too far from you
Know that I feel the same way
And that, again, we'll make it through
I'll be waiting for you right here
With my arms held open wide
Remember we are always together
For we share the same heart
And for two lovers such as us
We are never far apart
— Dan Stults

Sometimes I get all contemplative and try to picture what Dan would have done if I had died. He would still have to go to work. There would be no life insurance from me for him to fall back on. India would need some sort of daily babysitter for him to work, probably his mom. That would be more work for her. The house would be in shambles. I wonder if he would go to counseling. You would think he would, because he should know better, but he was never very good at taking care of himself.

I wonder what he would say about me on Facebook. Not a lot, I think. Not because he didn't love me as much, he just wasn't a "share my feelings with the public" kind of guy. But I never thought I was either, until this happened.

I wonder how he would cope. A lot differently than me, I'm sure. He wouldn't go out and try to do a million things. He wouldn't constantly be surrounded by friends and family. Not that they wouldn't try, but I think he would push them away. He was a solitary soul. Being around people didn't comfort him like it does me. I think he would build a fortress around the house and hide in it with India. They would keep to themselves, missing me on their own. Maybe that would have been better for her. She was forced to adopt many of my coping skills instead of coping in ways that she prefers, in ways that Dan would have preferred.

I don't think Dan would be so mad at God, he wasn't that way. He had more faith than I do. He was always allowing God to take control. I think he would have written about me, maybe in a blog, or maybe in a children's fairy tale where I would forever be a princess. He definitely would have written with more metaphor and existentialism than I do. I just tell it like it is.

It is hard for me to see past my own grief or India's grief. That is all I can focus on. I know other people grieve him, though. How could they not? He was out to save the world and he was making a dent. One of the biggest places he made an impact was at his work. Dan worked as the administrator of a mental health facility. He worked with mentally ill adults who have been all but given up on.

It's not exactly what Dan wanted to do; he wanted to help teenagers and families. However, always true to form, in grad school he procrastinated until the very end before getting an internship, and the only one left was the one nobody wanted:

mentally ill adults in residential treatment. While he was in that internship, he discovered how overlooked and under-served this population group was, and he was on a mission to fix it. He was making a career out of it. He wanted to revolutionize the mental health system.

I couldn't bear to call his boss and tell him that he had died. My dad did it for me. My dad called someone he didn't even know to tell them that Dan was dead. I don't know what he said or how that conversation went. I'm sure it wasn't pretty. Then, his boss had to tell Dan's staff and residents what had happened. I don't know how that conversation went either, but every staff member was at his funeral.

After Dan died, his colleagues put up a "wailing wall" for 40 days. It was a giant piece of butcher paper that ran down the hallway, for the staff and residents to write whatever they wanted to about Dan. After they took it down, they gave it to me. It had stuff on it like "Dan hated mint" and "Dan loved onion rings" with an empty package of onion rings taped to it. It also had a label from a Mountain Dew bottle taped onto it, because that was Dan's favorite drink. A bobblehead of Daryl from *The Walking Dead* was there, too; Dan and his boss loved talking about that show together. People had written poems, signed their names. Lots of "we will miss you" comments. Stories about cats. Jokes. It made me happy to see how much other people loved him, too. At the same time, it makes me deeply sad because he's not here. He is no longer helping these marginalized people. He is no longer revolutionizing the mental health system.

Dan's employer had a fountain made in Dan's honor and placed in the front yard of his workplace. Engraved into a rock just like the Lorax it says,

In loving memory of Dan Stults

Unless someone like you cares a whole awful lot,
nothing is going to get better, it's not.

They had a dedication for it and invited the family to come. Once again, I gave India the choice whether she wanted to come to Daddy's work and hear about him or go to school. She chose to go to school. His clients and staff talked about Dan and what he meant to them. They also told funny stories about him. His boss told a story of how, two days after he died, OSHA showed up for a safety inspection and he couldn't find any paperwork in Dan's office because Dan was the king of paper clutter.

After the ceremony everyone went inside for refreshments. His boss, one of his coworkers, my sister Pauline, and myself lingered by the fountain. My sister said something like we should have brought some ashes. I started to laugh, "Yeah, then he would be stuck at work forever!" Wait, this was a great idea. We should have brought some ashes. Wait! I did. I keep ashes in my car. His boss also smiled and thought this was a great joke on Dan, so I sent Pauline to my car to get the ashes. We spread them around the fountain. Now a part of him is always at work.

The spring after Dan died, I got a text from his boss. His company was building a new residential treatment center and he wanted my permission to name it after Dan.

> *It will serve folks with mental illness who are stepping*
> *down from a higher level of care. The program's mission is*
> *to teach skills that will help people live more independent*
> *lives. It gives the most vulnerable in our system a chance. It*
> *reminds me of Dan.*

There is a house in Portland, Oregon called Stults House. It is a treatment facility for mentally ill adults who otherwise wouldn't have had a chance. It's named after my husband. If you walk inside the front door, there is a picture of him. Behind the picture is a giant Lorax, looking over him in approval. Dan is helping to give the marginalized a chance. That's what Dan wanted, to help people. He would not have wanted an entire facility named after him, however. He would have said that we were all being ridiculous, and that he didn't do anything all that great. He would have hated the attention, but he's not here, so he didn't get a vote.

One of my all-time favorite shows is *Buffy the Vampire Slayer.* If you've never seen it, go watch it. Right now. It is amazing. Dan loved it, too, and even wrote a few college essays about Buffy. One of the greatest, most truthful lines in the entire series is right before Buffy is about to die. (She comes back; my friends and I spent months wondering how we could get our hands on that spell and Willow the witch to perform it.) Buffy's sister, Dawn, is scared of Buffy leaving her, and Buffy says, "The hardest thing in this world is to live in it." Truer words have never been spoken. The hardest thing in this world is to live in it. I suppose, without realizing it, that was my goal for India and myself. We were going to live, no matter how hard it was. And that's what I set out to do.

It was more than a year after Dan's death, before it occurred to me that if I was too tired to do something, I could skip it. The first year was go, go, go. Try to be normal. The second year I stopped. I stopped doing everything I was "supposed" to do. I realized that I was doing too much, so I stopped. I tried to rest. I quit showing up for parties. I skipped weddings and funerals because I wasn't emotionally fit enough to handle them. If I made it to church once a month, I was impressed with myself. I took a lot of naps. A lot. I was always so tired. We moved houses, and that was a whole new level of emotional drain.

I guess I would say year three was better. I didn't miss Dan any less. I still miss him with every heartbeat. It was better in that we were more settled. We were learning how to deal with missing Dan. We were learning how to deal with our grief. In a way, we were finally accustomed to our grief. We had our new house and were settled into it. India had a great teacher and a terrific school year. Every once in a while, I could see the sparkle come back into her eye and I thought, "Oh, there you are." Occasionally, I could see what I called my "red headed fire" come back to me, and I would think, "Oh, there you are." India and I were both so very lost, for so very long. I think part of our sparkle and fire will always be lost now. It went with Dan, but some of it is still here. It just takes a lot to find it.

Will that mean I'm healed? I hate that word. What does it mean to be healed? I talked about it with my therapist for a while, and then she asked me what I thought it would mean. I said, "For me to say something like, 'Oh, Dan and I used to always do such and such,' and smile at the good memory, then carry on with what I was doing and to NOT feel like I was being stabbed in the heart repeatedly."

She gave a very good answer. "That may never happen."

"Exactly," I said. "You see my dilemma."

So, now what? What do I do? We are kicking ass, and I miss Dan so much that I don't know how I can breathe. I am happy, and I am inconsolably sad. I told my therapist that being happy without Dan is wrong. She thought that was funny. She seems to think it's possible to be happy without the love of your life. I don't know how to describe the limbo we are in. How can I be happy when my soulmate is gone and all I want in the whole world is to touch him again? How can I be sad when my Baby Girl smiles at me, with freckles on her nose and her Daddy's eyes and says, "You're the best Mommy in the whole world"? I don't know. I don't know how I can be happy and sad at the same time, but I know it's possible, because I am. All the time.

I'm sure you have heard the phrase "it takes a village to raise a child". I have always believed that. You can't do it alone; even happily married couples can't raise a child without help sometimes. What I didn't know, and what I don't think anyone knows, is that it takes way more than a village to get someone through grief. It takes an entire freaking city. It takes a thriving metropolis. It takes so many different kinds of people to walk through grief with someone. To quote *We're Going on a Bear Hunt*, "You can't go over it, you can't go under it, you have to go through it." The problem is no one on this planet has the emotional capacity to go through it with you, even if they have gone through it themselves. As a griever you need so much, and it is impossible for one person to do all that with you. You need different people for different things.

You need besties that you can text at 3:00 in the morning with the phrase, "Dan sucks." They all reply with, "Yeah, he does," but they know that you are crying because you miss him so much, and what they are saying is that they are here with you. They tell you, "Whatever you are feeling is okay," and they feel it with you.

You need other besties that calmly and lovingly say, "You're not really mad at Dan. You're just missing him and are mad at the situation."

You need friends that can remind you, "Dan would have given up heaven to stay here with you and India, if he had any choice at all."

You need a dad who will go pick up ashes from the funeral home with you. "Then we can go out to lunch. Yay! I love Daddy–Daughter day," He tells you with a weak smile. It hurts him to see his daughter in so much pain.

You need sisters that come wake you up at 6:30 AM with coffee.

You need sisters that you can call at 10:00 PM and say, "The hamster got out and is lost in the house," knowing they will be over momentarily to help you find it.

You need in-laws who say without hesitation, "Move in with us. We will take care of you."

You need therapists who have a vested interest in you and want to go through this with you.

You need people who will drive 20 minutes to your house just to spend two minutes helping you move a bookshelf.

You need teachers who understand your kid and will fight for her to succeed.

You need old ladies at church who threaten to come beat your door down if they don't hear from you.

You need friends that take you to get a pedicure every month because they don't want to go alone.

You need "anonymous" people to leave Christmas presents on your doorstep and send you things through Amazon.

Rarely do people have such a thriving metropolis. Most of the time, all they have is a tiny village. Sometimes they don't even have that; they are out in the middle of nowhere, completely and utterly alone. I have a pastor friend, Cathy, who has seen lots and lots of grief; more grief than anyone should have to see. She told me once, "What I've found with grief is that you need enough people. You, Jenny, are the only person I have ever met that might just have enough people." I agree. I might have just enough people on my side, walking through this with me. I have enough people so that each person only has to walk with me a little way before passing the baton to someone else. I live in a freaking metropolis of friends and family. I always have.

I am not lucky that Dan died. That is asinine. Never tell anyone they are lucky when their loved one has just died. However, I am lucky that when tragedy struck, when I knew I couldn't go on, my metropolis took turns carrying me.

> *When you can't run, you crawl. And when you can't crawl, when you can't do that, well...you find someone to carry you.*

— Firefly

I had a friend message me, "My friend's husband just died, and she has two little kids. What can I do?"

Another message from a friend, "My friend's husband died. What can I say that isn't completely stupid? What can I do for her?"

I had a friend from high school die of cancer. I messaged her husband, whom I had never met. I told him I was sorry that his wife had died, that I always liked her, and that my husband had also died. Then I told him about our local support group for children who have lost parents. I also told him that I am no longer afraid to talk about death, the way many in our society are. So, if he had any questions, he could feel free to ask me because I wasn't scared. I can talk about death.

Without signing up for it, because no one in their right mind would ever do such a thing, I have become a sort of grief guru to the people that know me. I think maybe it is because when Dan died, all my walls came crumbling down. I was standing naked in front of an entire auditorium and I wasn't going to get clothes anytime soon, so I went with it. I talked about my pain. I posted about it on Facebook. I blogged about it. I wrote a book about it. I told everybody how life was for me: how much it hurt, how broken I was. I didn't care anymore about putting on a happy face. Furthermore, I didn't want to. My soulmate was dead at 36. It fucking hurts. It is the worst pain imaginable, it is even beyond imagination. I was not about to smile and pretend I was okay, because I wasn't.

People are not afraid to come to me with questions regarding death. I am asked far too often (because people die far too often) when someone they know dies, "What can I do?"

I usually tell them, "Go over there and do the damn dishes." I think a lot of times people who ask me that are looking for a more sophisticated answer. They want to know what they can say to their loved one to make the pain go away. I don't have an answer to that, because there is no answer. You cannot make their pain go away. Nothing you say is going to make them feel better, unless you said, "I have a way to bring someone back from the dead." I'm pretty sure they would be interested in that, and while you're at it, please share that information with me because I am interested in it, too. If you can't do that, just be there with them. Show up, sit next to them. Stare at the wall with them. That's the best you can do.

Is that my purpose, then? Dan died so that I could talk to other people about death? No offense, other people, but I am a selfish human being and talking to other people about grief is not worth it. I would rather he hadn't died. I would rather live in ignorant bliss, scared of conversations about death, but with a living husband. I want to be like everyone else, but I'm not. India's not. We are different now. Once you are in the club you never get out of the club. So, I took that huge gap that divided us from the normal world, and I tried to use it.

> I believe memories are more precious than many, if not most things, in this life.
> — Dan Stults

I never considered myself a writer, because I wasn't. I didn't like writing at all; it was not my thing. Dan was a wonderful writer and quite enjoyed it. That was good enough for me. He could write enough for both of us. But he died. Then I had all these huge emotions, and no one to talk to about them. One of the worst things in grief is not having the person you talk to about everything there, to talk about their death with.

I was scrolling the internet one night, looking for online grief groups. I wanted someone that I could talk to about grief at 3:00 AM when I was still awake. I stumbled on a website entitled "Refuge in Grief: Grief Support That Doesn't Suck". Well, that I could get behind. The site was owned by a woman named Megan Devine. I started reading her blogs. Then I discovered she had a class called "Writing Your Grief", where you write about your grief, alongside other grieving people. It's all online, and you can do it at 3:00 in the morning. It called to me. I don't know why, but it called to me. I needed to take this class.

"I'm not a writer; I'm not even sure why I'm here," is how I introduced myself in the online class. I wasn't a writer, but I started writing anyway because I didn't know what else to do. I thought that maybe, if I could write all these thoughts down, I would be able to sleep, and I wouldn't stay up all night thinking about them. If I could just get them out of my head, maybe I could sleep.

The class did exactly that. I would write, late at night when I would rather have been sleeping but couldn't. Many nights after writing about our grief topic, I could close my computer and go to sleep. It didn't always work, but it worked often. It is a great class; I highly recommend it, but it only lasted a month.

"Now what do I do?" I asked my therapist when the class was over.

"Why don't you start a blog?" she said. If I had had a drink in my mouth, I am certain I would have spit it out all over her.

"Because I'm not actually a writer. My spelling and grammar are horrible. I would have flunked out of college if I didn't have Dan to correct my papers for me. I have nothing useful to say. Nobody is going to read my 3:00 AM rantings about my dead husband."

"Who cares?" she replied. "No one has to read it. You don't even have to make it public if you don't want to. It's just a way for you to get your emotions out."

I guess I could give it a try. I decided to make it public, because I had nothing to hide. Dan was dead, it sucks, and I didn't care who knows it. My first blog was titled "My Therapist Told Me to Start a Blog" and then I went on to explain why. I started the blog about a year after Dan died. I wrote nightly, weekly, three times a week, whenever I couldn't sleep. To quote the musical *Hamilton*:

"I wrote my way out." I wrote my way out of grief. I am writing my way out of grief. Grief never ends, so I don't expect my writing will ever end.

"I wrote everything down far as I could see." All I could see was grief. That's all there was all around me: huge enormous grief, so I wrote it all down.

"I wrote my way out of hell." That's for sure. Grief is its own very special kind of hell, so I wrote about that too.

I discovered so many things through my writing. I discovered that I have a voice and I do have something to say. I discovered that writing can help me deal with my grief. I discovered that I am not alone. I discovered that what I have to write actually affects other people, and even helps some of them. I discovered that I like writing. I even missed it when I didn't get an opportunity to write for a few days. I discovered that I want to write my story, that I want to share my grief experience. I discovered that I am willing to and okay with talking about my grief, which many people aren't, so I can share my story for those who are not able to.

Some days I say to myself, "I must have gone completely crazy. I'm not a writer, I'm certainly not any good at it. Nobody is going to want to read my book. This grief thing has made me completely nuts." But other times, I can hear Dan's voice in my head.

"You got this, Jennifer. You got this."

I started this book with the quote "Death cannot stop true love." I told you I hated that quote, because it wasn't true in the end. Death is exactly what stopped our true love. But I had completely forgotten about the rest of the quote. The entire sentence is, "Death cannot stop true love. It can only delay it for a while." Oh, there it is. Dan Stults, my true love, my soulmate, death cannot stop our love. It has delayed it for a while, until I see you again in heaven. No matter what happens, Dan, no matter what other love I find, I will never love anyone as I loved you.

I can't wait to see you again; it's only a matter of time.

CHAPTER 17:

I'll Never Forget the First Time I Saw Your Face

∞ ∞ ∞

In walks the happy ending! Wait what? That's not how this story goes. I was prepared to end my book here, with no real ending, because there wasn't one. You can't tie grief up in a nice little bow. You can't live happily ever after without your soulmate.

> *Life's not a song; Life isn't bliss. Life is just this. It's living. You'll get along. The pain that you feel. You only can heal. By living. You have to go on living. So, one of us is living.*
>
> *— Buffy the Vampire Slayer*

That's what I was prepared to do. Just go on living, just so one of us is living.

Three years and two months after Dan died, I went out of town for the weekend. Luckily for me, my best friend Stacie came, too. We were in a hotel room, with nothing to do, and quite a bit of wine. My therapist is always telling me I should drink more, and this is what comes of it.

Stacie said, "We should sign you up for online dating!" She is the friend who always knows what to do; we joke that if Stacie tells you to do something, you do it, because she is always right.

"Okay, I guess," I agreed, and we signed me up, while drinking more wine. I was reluctant. I knew for a fact that I would never ever find anyone like Dan, so why even try? I believe in soulmates. I believed that once you found yours, that was it. I had clearly found mine. I had had my turn. I didn't get another, even if he died.

Furthermore, I wasn't about to settle. I had it too good with Dan. He treated me like a queen, I would not settle for anything less, and in my mind anyone who wasn't Dan was less.

Widow support groups are full of horror stories, about new boyfriends who don't or won't understand; boyfriends who ask widows to take the pictures of their husbands down, or not talk about their husbands so much, or at all. Widows have said things like, "My new boyfriend is moving in, so I have to get rid of all my dead husband's stuff." And those are some of the tamest stories I've heard. Hell to the NO! I would not be doing that, in any way shape or form. Screw that, and anyone who even thinks about asking me to erase Dan would be kicked to the curb. I would do whatever I wanted to regarding my dead husband, including (but not limited to) having six pictures of us kissing on the wall in my room, talking about him incessantly to anybody in ear shot, telling his daughter every single thing I can think of about him whenever it pops into my head, and carrying a small container of his ashes around in my car.

My criteria assured me that this dating thing was never going to happen. He didn't exist. A man that would be okay with kissing me one minute and listening to me cry over my dead husband the next minute did not exist. I was sure of it. It was going to be awful. I would go on one terrible date after another, never finding anyone who could come close to measuring up to Dan. That was what I was in for, so why was I even trying? My bestie Shirley said, "No, Jenny, dating is going to be easy for you. It has to be. You've been through way too much crap. God has to give this one to you." I laughed at her. Ha! That's exactly why it was going to be awful. Life wasn't exactly going smoothly these days. There was no way that dating would go smoothly. I had my true love. You don't get another. I was done.

As my besties explained it, however, I didn't have to go looking for true love or soul mates. It was perfectly fine just to find someone to go to the movies with. Okay, I thought. I could do that. It would be nice to have dinner and some grown up conversation. So, I signed up for online dating. Do you know what became of it? Nothing, absolutely nothing. I hated it.

I messaged people that I thought seemed interesting. 99% of the time, I got no response. I had online conversations with a few people, but nothing was noteworthy. I wrote on my profile that I was widowed, that my husband was a great man and a fantastic father, and that they were going to have to be okay with that or I wasn't interested. My therapist said I was "challenging people." I said, "Damn right I am. If they can't deal with me having a dead husband, then to hell with them."

One day I messaged a man. His name was Justin, and I was giving him crap about one of his profile pictures. I didn't care. I wasn't invested, and if he was offended, he wasn't good enough to go to the movies with. But he gave me crap back. That started our conversation. We talked and talked and talked online. He told me his story, and I told him mine. Before ever meeting him in person, I told him how I watched my husband die. I told him I still loved Dan. He said, "Of course you do. why wouldn't you?" We talked about simple things, like what beach near us is the best and how we like our coffee. We talked about complicated things like children.

Soon, it became clear that Justin was good enough to go out to eat with. We scheduled a breakfast date for his next day off. It was the first date I had been on since Dan died. I will never forget when I walked around the corner of that restaurant and saw him. He got up to give me a hug, like he had always known me. Like we were old friends. We sat down. Justin grabbed my hand and looked into my eyes, and I immediately thought, "Oh. Oh right, this. I know this." He tells a similar story. We connected, immediately, on a very deep level, like we had always known each other. Some might say we knew one another in a past life, but I don't believe in past lives. We simply understood one another.

Justin is not a cure for grief. He cannot fix me, and he tells me often that he is not trying to fix me. He is not Dan. No one will ever be Dan. He does, however, bring out my grief in new ways I never considered before.

One of the first times we kissed, we were sitting next to each other. It was a whole new experience, a different type of kiss. It didn't feel the way it did when Dan and I kissed. They are wholly different. Both are wonderful, but they are different. After he kissed me, I instinctively laid my head on his chest. Guess what? He had something Dan didn't have. Justin had a fucking heartbeat. Thump, Thump, Thump, Thump. I could hear his heart beating. He had a heartbeat.

That triggered an immediate panic attack. I jumped up and moved away, tears pouring out of my eyes. I was breathing fast, anxious, scared. I covered my head in my hands and tried to calm down, but it wasn't working. Justin knew something had triggered my reaction. He very gently scooted toward me and asked me to tell him what was going on. For a brief moment, I wondered how to explain without scaring him away. Then I thought, nope, screw that. I am telling him exactly what happened and if he can't handle it, then we are not as connected as I thought. I looked at him and then looked away. I tried to take a deep breath, I don't know if I was successful.

Quietly, I said, "The last time I put my head on somebody's chest, it was Dan's chest and I was looking for a heartbeat. I couldn't hear his heartbeat. I put my head on your chest and you have a heartbeat."

He scooted closer and put his arm around me. I cried more. After a few minutes, he said, "I can't possibly imagine how hard this is for you. I know I can't fix it either, no matter how much I want to. But I can be here for you. I can hold you while you cry, I can hold your hand and just be here." I cried for probably another half an hour. That was our second date.

A couple weeks later I messaged my dad and my siblings, "Nobody freak out!!! I may have started dating someone." Most of them freaked out, despite my warning. Especially my dad. He wanted to know how we met.

"Stacie made me sign up for online dating."

"God bless Stacie."

A few weeks later, I officially posted a picture of us on Facebook and introduced him as my boyfriend. It sounds silly and childish, but I was nervous about doing that. Not because of him, but because of me. I knew already what an amazing guy he was, and I knew I wanted him in our lives. But it meant that I was admitting, to myself and to the world, that I was wrong. I did have room in my heart for someone other than Dan. No, that's not the right wording. It's more like along with Dan. I have room in my heart for someone along with Dan. I didn't think that was possible, but Justin showed me it was. He also made room in his heart for Dan, which was key.

He adores India. She is still working on getting used to him, and that's okay. We all knew it would be hard. She goes through times where she has fun with him and they laugh and joke. Then she has times where she is literally pushing him out the door because she doesn't want him at our house. In those times, I try to apologize for my child's rude behavior. Justin always stops me and says, "You have nothing to apologize for, I know this is hard for her. She has every right to feel this way."

Justin came to Thanksgiving. It was the first big family event he attended. It could have been awkward, having my boyfriend at Thanksgiving and not my dead husband, although technically my dead husband was there also. But Thanksgiving was good. I don't think it could have gone any more smoothly. Justin cooked our turkey, and India helped him prep it. They pulled out the guts and washed it. India played with its body parts and named it Frederick. They tied up its legs and gave it a bath in boiling oil. They laughed India made fun of Justin and teased him. They had a great time.

Since Thanksgiving had gone so well, I invited Justin to Christmas. I told India, and a chill entered the room. I looked in her eyes. She has Dan's beautiful, bright, blue eyes. Just as Dan's did, they turn red almost instantly when she is upset or not feeling well. They welled up with tears. Rage swept over her body.

"HE IS NOT COMING TO CHRISTMAS," she shouted, and kicked my foot in anger.

"Yeah, baby I think he is. It's okay. We had a great time at Thanksgiving." Her fists were clenched and her knuckles were turning white.

"Mommy he is not coming. Say he's not coming!"

"No, I'm not going to say that."

She screamed and buried her head in the couch. Then she started to yell. "I don't like him, Mommy! I don't like him. He's stupid. I wish it would go back to the way it was. Just me and Mommy. He can't come to Christmas. HE'S NOT FAMILY! He can't open presents with us. He can't sit on the couch and watch me and my cousins open presents!"

Now we were getting somewhere. My brain flashes back to the Christmases in The Before. Dan and I would sit on the couch, his arm around me, the other adults doing likewise, while all the kids sat on the floor and opened presents. India would look up at us and smile because we were smiling at her opening presents.

Then I had a thought. I might as well get it out; she can't get any madder.

"Being around Justin makes you miss Daddy more, doesn't it?"

"YEEEEEESSSSSSS," she wailed.

"Because you remember all the fun we used to have with Daddy, when Justin is around?"

"SO?" she said, defiant. I get it, I so get it.

"Yeah, Baby Girl, I understand. I felt that way too when I first started hanging out with him. He does make me miss Daddy more sometimes." She looked at me like I'm an idiot. To her, this was simple.

"So why do you still hang around with him?" she asked. The rage was quieting, and she really wanted to know the answer. What could I tell her? That it's all kinds of complicated? I couldn't not? I was drawn to him? I like him?

"You know I love Daddy like I have never loved anyone else. I will always, always love Daddy, no matter what. He is Daddy and that does not change. But I learned that it's okay to like someone else, too. It's okay to like Justin and do fun things with him and have good times. That does not mean we stop loving Daddy. We will never ever, ever stop loving Daddy. You can do both, Baby Girl. It's okay to do both. You can like hanging out with Justin and you will still love Daddy more than anything in the world. It's okay to do both."

She started to cry. A quiet cry, not a raging screaming cry.

"But I don't want to."

241

I went to my room. I crawled under the covers, too mentally drained to ever move again. I called Justin, crying, and told him what happened.

"That's great, Jen, I'm so glad. India is processing her emotions. That is so, so good. Now we can figure out how to help her through this."

Since we had this conversation, India is more open to the idea of Justin. Now, when he comes over for dinner, she just rolls her eyes at him instead of saying, "Go home, I don't want you here." I have even caught her starting conversations with him and asking him questions. India likes Justin. I think she likes him a lot. She doesn't want to. Somewhere in her head she thinks that she is betraying Daddy. I get that. Sometimes I worry about that, too. She's doesn't quite understand that she can like Justin and we can do fun things, and she can still love Daddy. She doesn't have to choose one or the other, she can do both. It's a hard lesson for an 11-year-old to comprehend. It's a hard lesson for an adult to comprehend, but it's true.

We talk about Dan so much. I think I mention him every day, and Justin is fine with that. He likes looking at the pictures on my walls, and he asks me to tell him the story behind them. He tells me that Dan must have been a wonderful husband and father. I respond with, "Yes, he was," and that doesn't intimidate Justin. One night we were sitting on the couch, he had his arm around me, and we were talking about a little beach town near us and the fun tourist things to do there. One place in particular has a beautiful view point. I sighed heavily and became quiet.

"Are you having a memory?" he gently asked.

"Yeah," I said as a small tear came down my eye.

"Would you like to share it with me?" I would.

"The last time I was in that town, we had gone there for the weekend to celebrate our 15-year wedding anniversary. We went up to that view point and watched the sunset. It was so beautiful, it was so perfect. We spent the whole weekend together, going to museums and seeing the sights. We had the best time together. Less than six months later, he was dead."

Justin wrapped his arms around me and gently kissed the back of my head.

"I am so glad you got to spend your last anniversary with him having such a great weekend. That is a beautiful memory." We sat for a while as he held me.

I was talking to Justin on the phone one night. We were discussing the coincidental events that brought us together. We both agree that it wasn't really coincidence. It was fate, providence, God. We were put together for a reason. I truly believe that. Justin truly believes that. It always gives me pause, though. If we were put together for a reason then certain life events happened for a reason, or rather on purpose. I don't know if I can accept that. In the middle of a cute conversation about how we met I started to cry.

"What is it, darlin'? You can tell me."

"I know I can, I just can't say the words." I gulp, I try to breathe, but my crying is getting in the way. "Do you...do you...Do you think God let Dan die so that I could meet you?" I burst into uncontrollable sobs.

"No, no I don't, of course I don't."

I was sobbing. I knew that was what he would say, but I had to hear it anyway, I had to let the thoughts in my head finally come out of my mouth. I can't catch my breath, I am crying so hard, I wish Dan were here.

"I miss Dan," I cried.

"I know you do, of course you do, how couldn't you? Jen...Jenny...Jennifer...do you need me to come over?"

"Yes."

Justin got up late at night and came over. He works early in the morning, and he came over. I curled up into him and sobbed. I sobbed and sobbed and sobbed.

"I'm so glad you're here...I miss Dan...Thank you for coming over...why did Dan have to die...why couldn't he just keep breathing...I keep breathing, it's not fair," and he held me. He held me and let me cry. He held me while I missed my husband. He didn't say I needed to get it together. He didn't say I should be over Dan. He didn't ask me to stop talking about this. He knows I still love Dan and tells me I have every right to, because I do. He holds me and lets me cry. It makes the crying not so harsh when you're being held. He somehow understands.

To quote my friend Jill again, "I sort of think there's no purpose in people dying. God doesn't let people die to achieve his plan. People just die. and then he uses that to achieve parts of his plan. I don't think God took him. I think God can and will do amazing things in the wake of Dan's death, but God didn't take Dan."

Occasionally, Justin says that he wishes we had met years ago, and I reply with the smart-ass comment, "Well, I was busy." He wasn't ready either. He was living his life, and I was living mine. If we had crossed paths, we wouldn't even have noticed each other. We weren't ready then, but we are ready now. God took my pain, and Justin's pain too, and did something amazing with it. He put us together, and we needed each other so badly.

The Christmas before Dan died, he gave me a small patio set. A round table and two chairs. It was exactly what I wanted.

"Then we can sit outside on warm summer nights and sip wine and watch our kids play," I told him when I was giving him Christmas ideas. That is exactly what I wanted it for, to sit next to my love and watch our kids play in the yard. That's exactly why he got it for me. He wanted that too. He died before I even got it out of the box. We never got there. Eventually I set it up, but I never sat in it. I had no one to sit next to now.

One summer night, Justin was over with his kids. All the kids were running around the yard, screaming and laughing. We were walking around sipping wine.

"Here, let's sit down," he suggested as we got to my patio set. We did, and thought nothing of it. We sipped wine and watched the kids play in the yard. Later that night I called him crying. I told him about Dan getting me that patio set, and how we never got to use it.

"Tonight was the first time I sat in it. Tonight, I did exactly what I wanted that patio set for. I sat and sipped wine, while I watched the kids play. I just never thought I would be doing it with you. I always thought I would be doing it with Dan." He understood, he got it. He held me through the phone while I cried over Dan.

I like to think Justin and Dan would be friends. They are different people. Dan was an intellectual but couldn't fix a damn thing. Justin can fix anything but isn't real big on reading. They both have a love for nature and animals. They both have the sweetest caring hearts. They are both very chivalrous. They both adore India and me. I imagine when we catch up to Dan in heaven they will shake hands and hug.

Justin will say, "Thank you, Dan, for taking such great care of my Jen."

Dan will say, "Thank you, Justin, for taking such great care of my Jennifer."

Justin says they will hug and we will all walk away together holding hands. There will be no animosity or jealousy. It doesn't work like that. I don't know what is going to happen with Justin in the long term, but he has already helped me realize something huge. Without telling his story, which is not mine to tell, I will say he did not experience love the way I did. I was loved so well, possibly more than anyone I know of. My grief has been all about my loss, India's loss, the world's loss. Amazing love was lost when Dan so suddenly left this world. I was certain no one would ever love me the way Dan did, and therefore I could never be in love again.

That is half true. No one will ever love me the way Dan did. Dan was Dan and no one will ever be him. It was all about what was lost. I didn't take into account what I had to give. I didn't think I had anything left to give. I didn't take anyone else into account. I didn't know that Justin was out there, and I didn't know he was looking for me to be able to show him love, in a way he had never experienced before.

Recently, I have realized that Dan gave me enough love that I can show it to other people. I loved Dan. I loved Dan with every piece of my soul. I still do. Justin knows that, and he knows that he is not in competition with a dead guy. Love doesn't work like that. I can show Justin love that he has never known because Dan loved me so fiercely, because I have experienced true love. I can help him see how beautiful and wonderful and fun real love can be. Dan showed me that. The best way to honor Dan is to share my love with others.

> *"People often want to replace their sadness with happiness, but as an existentialist, I am in favor of sadness. I am also a big proponent of joy-joy in spite of sadness, joy that is bigger than sadness. How arrogant it would be for me to think that I could actually eliminate someone's sadness and replace it with happiness, life in a fallen world will not allow such a thing. But if I can help someone find meaning and purpose in their sadness, if I can help them grow from the sadness and learn to cope with the sadness and still enjoy the image of God inside them, then I have brought them joy."*
> *-Dan Stults*

Made in the USA
Coppell, TX
11 April 2022